THE ⟡ TIMES

Style
and
Usage
Guide

Compiled by Tim Austin
Introduced by Robert Thomson

TIMES BOOKS

HarperCollins*Publishers*
77–85 Fulham Palace Road
Hammersmith
London W6 9JB

The HarperCollins website address is
www.**fire**and**water**.com

First published 2003

Reprint 10 9 8 7 6 5 4 3 2 1 0

© Times Newspapers Ltd 2003

ISBN 0 00 714505 5

The Times is a registered trademark of Times Newspapers Ltd

British Library Cataloguing in Publication Data
A catalogue record for this book is available from
the British Library

Text design by Clare Crawford

Printed and bound in Great Britain by
Clays Ltd, St Ives plc

Editor's Preface

The word "style" has taken on a general meaning far removed from the pages of a newspaper or the galley proof of a book, but that has not lessened the importance of the concept for the specialist or the linguistically curious. This new edition of *The Times Style and Usage Guide* aims to incorporate the traditional virtues of "style" and the value of contemporary usage. Words and phrases move in and out of fashion, sometimes for good reason and sometimes because of institutional misuse. This upgraded and expanded guide aims to be a ready reference source for any writer or reader, professional or casual, who cares enough about the language to use it correctly.

The word "guide" is also in need of examination. We do not intend this to be a fire and brimstone book – all ye who fail to follow our scripture to the letter will be eternally damned and inevitably wrong. Style is a template of the times, not an utterly irrevocable rule. That is not to suggest we are in favour of anarchy, but we do allow exceptions. Quoted conversation should be as real as the spoken word and not made unreal by cleaning unsightly words or structures. A columnist is not a reporter and a writer of fiction is not a business journalist seeking enough precision to make corporate accounts comprehensible.

We welcome all users of the language to this Style Guide and encourage feedback from readers who are convinced that we have failed to cull the archaic or that we have tried too hard to be "stylish".

Robert Thomson
Editor, *The Times*
London 2003

A

a, **an** use *a* before all words beginning with a vowel or diphthong with the sound of *u* (as in unit) – a eulogy, a European etc; but use *an* before unaspirated *h* – an heir, an honest woman, an honour; also, prefer an hotel to a hotel, an historic to a historic, an heroic rather than a heroic

abattoir

Abbey National is a bank, not a building society. Others that have similarly changed status include the Halifax, the Woolwich, the Alliance & Leicester etc. *See* building societies

abbreviations prefer not to abbreviate Professor to Prof, Father to Fr etc. *See* military ranks

abbreviated negatives (can't, don't, shan't etc, plus similar abbreviations such as I'll, you're) should be discouraged in all text except in direct quotes, though in chatty pieces such as the Diary and some features they are permissible when the full form would sound pedantic

Abdication cap with specific reference to Edward VIII's; in general sense, use l/c. *See* Royal Family

Aboriginal (singular, noun and adjective), and **Aborigines** (plural), for native Australian(s); **aboriginal** (l/c) for wider adjectival use

Acas the Advisory, Conciliation and Arbitration Service

accents give French, Spanish, Portuguese, German, Italian and Ancient Greek words their proper accents and diacritical marks; omit in other languages unless you are sure of them. Accents are not necessary in headlines. With Anglicised words, no need for accents in foreign words that have taken English nationality (hotel, depot, debacle, elite, regime etc), but keep the accent when it makes a crucial difference to pronunciation – café, communiqué, fête, fiancée, mêlée, émigré, pâté, protégé; also note vis-à-vis, façade. *See* foreign words

Achilles' heel, but Achilles tendon. *See* apostrophes

acknowledgement

acoustic(s) (not accoustics)

Act and **Bill** cap whether fully identified or not

actor, actress. *See* feminine designations

Actuary the Government Actuary takes caps

AD, BC note that AD comes before the date, eg, AD35; BC comes after, 350BC. With *century*, both are used after, eg, 3rd century BC/AD

adapter (person who adapts); **adaptor** (plug, device)

Addenbrooke's Hospital, Cambridge

addresses no commas in 1 Pennington Street etc; and do not abbreviate Street. *See* postal addresses

adidas (l/c) policy is now to allow companies the styles they wish to follow. *See* AXA, BUPA, easyJet etc

adjectives avoid clichéd adjectives as in *long-felt* want, *serious* danger, *widespread* concern, *substantial* majority etc

Adjutant-General takes the hyphen

Administration (US)

Admiral do not abbreviate to Adm Jones etc except in lists; subsequent mentions, the admiral. *See* Armed Forces special section (page 14)

admissible, inadmissible (not –able)

ad nauseam (not ad nauseum)

adrenalin (prefer to adrenaline)

adult magazines avoid this circumlocution; say pornographic magazines instead

adverbs when they are used to qualify adjectives, the joining hyphen is rarely needed, eg, heavily pregnant, classically carved, colourfully decorated. But in some cases, such as well-founded, ill-educated, the compound looks better with the hyphen. The best guidance is to use the hyphen in these phrases as little as possible or when the phrase would otherwise be ambiguous

adviser (never advisor)

affect, effect as a verb, to affect means to produce an effect on, to touch the feelings of, or to pretend to have or feel (as in affectation); to effect is to bring about, to accomplish. If in doubt, always consult the dictionary

Afghan (noun or adjective); an **afghani** (l/c) is a unit of currency, not a person

African Union (AU abbreviated) replaces (summer 2002) the Organisation of African Unity (OAU)

Afrikaans, the language; **Afrikaners**, the people

after almost invariably to be used rather than *following*. Also, beware of careless use in sentences such as "The British player won a place in the final after beating the seeded German". Say instead "... by beating the seeded German". *See* as, following

afterlife (one word)

ages normal style is Joe Brown, 33, a porter; and in this format, keep children's ages as figure for the sake of consistency, eg, "Emma Watson, 7, who …"; but "the seven-year-old child said …" (up to and including ten); occasional variations such as "Andrew Hunt, who is 74, said …" are also permissible. Note caps in **Ice Age**, **Stone Age**, the **Dark Ages** etc

ageing takes the middle "e" – as in **axeing**, **likeable**, **mileage**, **moveable**, **rateable**, **sizeable**, **unlikeable**, **unshakeable** etc. The most common exceptions are listed separately, eg, **unmistakable**

aggravate means to make (an evil or complaint) worse. It does not mean to annoy or irritate

AGM caps, but prefer *annual meeting* in text

agoraphobia (not agaro-, agra- etc)

Agriculture, Ministry/Minister of (not Department/Secretary) no longer exists, having been subsumed into the Department for Environment, Food and Rural Affairs. In historical contexts, the old Ministry of Agriculture may be abbreviated to MAFF

Aids (acquired immune deficiency syndrome) is *not* a disease, but a medical condition. Diseases that affect people who are HIV-positive may be called Aids-related diseases; but through custom and practice we can now afford to relax the rule

about *never* saying "died of Aids". *See* HIV

AIM, the Alternative Investment Market; keep caps in abbreviation

Air Accidents Investigation Branch (caps, and note Accidents)

airbase, **airstrip**, **airspace** (no hyphens); but *see* **air fares**, **air show**, **airstrikes**

air-conditioner, **air-conditioning** (hyphenate)

aircraft prefer to *planes* wherever possible. Remember that not all aircraft are jets – some are still turbo-prop. Also always avoid the American *airplanes*. *See* planes

aircraft names are italicised, as with ships' or locomotive names, eg, the *Enola Gay* (Hiroshima bomber). *See* locomotive, ships

aircraft types B52, F111 etc (no hyphens between letter and numbers)

aircraftman, **aircraftwoman** not aircraftsman etc. *See* Armed Forces special section (page 14)

air fares (two words, as rail fares, bus fares etc)

air force cap in full name such as Royal Air Force (thereafter the RAF), US Air Force (USAF), Brazilian Air Force (thereafter the air force, l/c); and l/c in adjectival use, eg, an air force raid. *See* Armed Forces special section (page 14)

Air Miles take care when to cap; the Air Miles scheme is run by BA and should usually be capped; but it can take the l/c if used in a general context

airports as a general rule for British airports, use the name of the city or town followed by l/c airport, eg, Manchester airport, Leeds/Bradford airport, even East Midlands airport, Luton airport; but *see* Heathrow, Gatwick, Stansted. Note at Heathrow, **Terminal 1, 2, 3, 4, 5** etc

air raid (two words, but *see* airstrikes)

air show (two words); cap when specific, eg, the Paris Air Show, the Farnborough Air Show

airstrikes one word in military sense, but air raids (two words)

air traffic control service. *See* National Air Traffic Services

akimbo use only with reference to arms (never legs). It means hands on the hips with elbows turned outwards

al- as the prefix to Arabic nouns (including names), prefer the *al-* to the *el-* form, except where the *el-* has become widely accepted

Albert Hall generally omit Royal

A level, no hyphen, but A-level results etc (hyphenate only when adjectival). A levels now embrace AS levels and A2s, and can still be used

as the generic phrase and in historical context. But use **O levels** (same hyphenation rules) now only in historical context. *See* GCSE, examinations

Al Fayed Mohamed Al Fayed is chairman of Harrods. His youngest brother Ali Fayed is deputy chairman of Harrods. Their brother Saleh Fayed is not a resident of the UK. The brothers should be spelt like this, with no variation. The late elder son was Dodi Fayed

Alfa Romeo

alibi not a general alternative to excuse; it means being elsewhere at the material time

al-Jazeera TV station in Qatar. *See* War on Terror

Allahu akbar (God is greatest)

allcomers (one word)

allege avoid the suggestion that the writer is making the allegation, so specify its source. Do not use *alleged* as a synonym of *ostensible*, *apparent* or *reputed*

Allende, Isabel the Chilean novelist (born in Lima, Peru) is the niece and goddaughter of the former Chilean President, Salvador Allende, *not* his daughter

All England Club home of the Wimbledon Championships (no hyphen)

All Hallows Eve (not Allhallows)

Allies cap the Allies in the Second World War context; generally, l/c **alliance**, as in the *Atlantic alliance*, Gulf War alliance etc

Allitt, Beverly the child-killer convicted in May 1993

all right never *alright*

All Souls College, Oxford (no apostrophe); *see* Oxford colleges

all-time avoid as in *all-time high*; use *highest* or *record high* instead

al-Qaeda Osama bin Laden's group. *See* War on Terror

alsatian (l/c, the German shepherd dog); wherever possible, l/c for breeds of dogs; but obvious exceptions include Yorkshire terrier. *See* dogs

alternative of two, **choice** of three or more

Alwaleed, Prince despite our usual style with Arabic names (l/c al, followed by hyphen and cap first letter of name) the Saudi investor and businessman Prince Alwaleed Bin Talal Bin Abdul Aziz prefers to style himself thus (though Prince Alwaleed is usually sufficient). His son is Prince Khalid Bin Alwaleed. *See* Arabic names, Saudi

al-Yamamah (oil-for-arms defence project); not Al Yamamah

Amateur Athletic Association (not Athletics)

Amazon.com (use initial cap)

Ambassador cap when specific, eg, the French Ambassador, thereafter the ambassador

ambience prefer to the French spelling *ambiance*

America(n)/US in general, try to use *American* as in "American cities, American food" etc; but US in headlines and in the context of government institutions, such as US Congress, US Navy, US military operation. Never use *America* when ambiguity could occur with Canada or Latin America. *See* United States

American spellings normally use the English spelling even with offices or institutions such as Secretary of Defense (change to Defence), American Federation of Labor (change to Labour), or with buildings, eg, the Lincoln Center (change to Centre); but Labor Day (which has no UK equivalent) is an exception. *See also* Pearl Harbor

America's Cup, the (yachting)

amid, not *amidst*; similarly **among**, not *amongst*

amok not *amock* or *amuck*

amphitheatres in classical context are oval or circular (eg, the Colosseum in Rome); do not confuse with theatres, which are semi-circular or horseshoe-shaped

Amsterdam treaty (l/c "t"), but the Treaty of Amsterdam (caps). *See* Maastricht

analog (in computer context); but keep analogue as in an analogous or parallel thing. *See* program

ancestor strictly means a person from whom another is directly descended, especially someone more distant than a grandparent. Do not use in the looser sense of predecessor; eg, Queen Elizabeth I is not the ancestor of the present Queen

Ancient Briton/Britain, Ancient Greek/Greece, Ancient Egyptian/ Egypt, Ancient Roman/Rome

Ancram, Michael (Tory politician); he is formally the Earl of Ancram, but he sits as an MP and we refer to him simply as Michael Ancram, or Mr Ancram. His daughters are Lady Clare Kerr and Lady Mary Kerr (not Ancram)

Andersen, the accountancy firm (no longer Arthur Andersen); the former Andersen Consulting is now **Accenture**

Andersen, Hans Christian (*not* Anderson)

aneurysm not aneurism

Anglesey (never Anglesea)

Anglicise, Anglophile (caps), **anglophone** (l/c)

Anglo-Irish agreement. *See* Ireland

angst (roman l/c)

animals beware the solecism "birds and animals"; say "birds and mammals" instead

animal names call an animal "he" or "she" if the sex is definitely known or if called by a masculine or feminine name (eg, Felix the cat had only himself to blame). But use "it" if sex is unspecified. On the racing pages, horses are always "he" or "she"

annexe (noun), but to **annex** (verb)

anoint not *annoint*

answerphone, or answering machine

Antarctic, Arctic (never *Antartic* etc)

antennae (plural of antenna) in zoological sense; **antennas** in radio or aerial sense

Anti-Ballistic Missile Treaty (all initial caps), ABM Treaty for short

Antichrist (initial cap)

anticipate not to be used for *expect*. It means to deal with, or use, in advance of, or before, the due time. To anticipate marriage is different from expecting to marry

antidepressant (noun or adjective), no hyphen

Antipodes, Antipodean cap A when referring to Australia and New Zealand

anti-Semitic, anti-Semitism

antisocial, anticlimax, antitrust

Anti-Terrorist Branch, Special Branch (caps); but police squads in most cases l/c, except **Flying Squad** and **Royalty and Diplomatic Protection Squad**

any more always two words

Apennines, Italy (not Appenines)

apostrophes with proper names/ nouns ending in s that are singular, follow the rule of writing what is voiced, eg, **Keats's poetry**, **Sobers's batting**, *The Times's* **style** (or *Times* **style**); and with names where the final "s" is soft, use the "s" apostrophe, eg, **Rabelais' writings**, **Delors' presidency**; plurals follow normal form, as **Lehman Brothers' loss** etc

Note that with Greek names of more than one syllable that end in "s", do not use the apostrophe "s", eg, **Aristophanes' plays**, **Achilles' heel**, **Socrates' life**, **Archimedes' principle**

Beware of organisations that have variations as their house style, eg, **St Thomas' Hospital**, where we must respect their whim

Also, take care with apostrophes with plural nouns, eg, **women's**, not womens'; **children's**, not childrens'; **people's**, not peoples', but *see* people

Use the apostrophe in expressions such as **two years' time**, **several hours' delay** etc

An apostrophe should be used to indicate the plural of single letters – **p's and q's**

apparatchik

appellations on news pages, though not on features and sport, almost every surname should be granted the courtesy of a title. The exceptions are: convicted offenders, the dead (but not the recently dead, except in obituaries), and – mostly in the arts, sports, books and diary sections – cases where common usage omits a title. On news pages, similarly, sportsmen, artists, authors, film stars, pop stars, actors etc should now normally **not** be referred to as Mr/Mrs/Ms etc, except in court cases or exceptional occasions where guilt would be implied by omitting the honorific.

General rules:

a. First mention, Herbert Palfry, Juliette Worth, subsequently Mr Palfry, Mrs/Miss/Ms Worth

b. Put the name first, then the age (if relevant), then the description; eg, Jane Fonda, 57, the American actress; **avoid the journalese construction "actress Jane Fonda"**

c. Avoid initials and middle initials (as in American names) unless the person is best-known thereby (eg, W. G. Grace, with full points)

d. Ms is nowadays fully acceptable when a woman wants to be called thus, or when it is not known for certain if she is Mrs or Miss

e. Dr is no longer confined to medical doctors; if a person has a doctorate from a reputable university, Dr is acceptable

f. Court proceedings: accused people should be accorded the appropriate title (Mr, Miss etc) – however guilty they may appear – after name and first name have been given at first mention; only convicted persons should be referred to by surname alone. But do be sensitive especially in murder cases, where the accused is given, for example, his "Mr"; the victim (despite the dead not usually being given a title) should here be accorded the courtesy of the title. Otherwise the stark contrast of, say, Mr X being accused of the murder of Dando, can appear gratuitously offensive

See also foreign names, titles, Armed Forces special section (page 14), Courts special section (page 47)

appendix plural appendices, but appendixes in anatomy

appraise means evaluate; **apprise** means inform. Never confuse

April Fool's Day, **April fool**, but **All Fools' Day**

Aqaba, Gulf of (Red Sea)

aqueduct (not aquaduct)

Arabic names always take care in this difficult area. But remember the basic rule of al-X (l/c al, with hyphen, before name; rarely use the el- form)

Arafat, Yassir (not Yasser)

arbitrate, **arbitration** do not confuse with *mediate, mediation*. An arbitrator hears evidence from different parties then hands down a decision; a mediator listens to the different arguments then tries to bring the parties to agreement

archaeologist, **archaeology**. *See* palaeontology

archbishops

a. **Anglican** archbishops and diocesan bishops in the UK: at first mention, the Archbishop of Barchester, the Most Rev John Smith; or the Bishop of Barchester, the Right Rev John Smith, but if a doctor, the Bishop of Barchester, Dr John Smith; subsequent references, the Archbishop (Bishop) (caps), or Dr Smith (if so entitled) – never Mr Smith;

b. The Archbishop of Canterbury is Primate of All England, the Archbishop of York is Primate of England;

c. Anglican bishops are consecrated, Roman Catholic bishops ordained;

d. **Roman Catholic** archbishops, at first mention: the Roman Catholic Archbishop of Liverpool, the Most Rev John X, subsequent mentions Archbishop X or the Archbishop; bishops, first mention the Roman Catholic Bishop of Plymouth, the Right Rev Christopher Y, thereafter Bishop Y or the Bishop, unless he has a doctorate, when he is Dr Y. *See* Churches special section (page 37)

Archer, Garath (not Gareth), England rugby player

Argentine is the adjective; an **Argentinian** is a person from Argentina (never the Argentine)

armada be careful with imprecise use of this word; it means a fleet of *armed* ships, so strictly should not be applied to any collection of boats or ships

Armageddon (cap)

armchair, deckchair (no hyphens)

Armed Forces, the (caps); also **the Services**

Armistice Day is not the same as Remembrance Sunday (unless November 11 falls on a Sunday). *See* two minutes' silence, Remembrance Sunday

Armstrong Siddeley (no hyphen)

Army cap in context of the British Army (thereafter the Army, capped), and foreign armies, as in the Belgian Army, the Swiss Army (but thereafter the army, l/c); and always l/c when used adjectivally, eg, an army helicopter. *See* Armed Forces special section (page 14)

Arran (Isle of), in the Firth of Clyde; but the **Aran Islands** (note one "r") off Co Galway in western Ireland, and **Aran Island** (singular)

off Co Donegal; and an **Aran sweater** etc

artefact do not use *artifact*

artistic knights with these, use only surname in their artistic contexts (eg, Rattle conducted the Berlin Philharmonic with panache), but full title in news stories with, for example, political or social contexts (eg, Sir Simon Rattle visited No 10 yesterday). Similarly, McKellen played Lear, but Sir Ian McKellen led the gay rights march

artistic movements cap Art Deco, Baroque, Classical, Neo-Classical, Cubist, Gothic, Impressionist, Minimalist, Modernist, Post-Modern, Pre-Columbian, Pre-Raphaelite, Rococo, Romantic, Surrealist etc in cultural contexts; but in wider general use, l/c, eg, "He had a surrealist sense of humour but a romantic nature"

Arts and Crafts movement

arts awards initial cap for titles of awards such as Best Actress, Best Film, Play of the Year etc

as beware of sloppy use in sentences such as "They were moved out as the blast tore open the building"; say simply "*after* the blast ..."

Asean (Association of South East Asian Nations): Indonesia, Singapore, Malaysia, Thailand, the Philippines, Brunei, Vietnam, Burma, Laos and Cambodia. *See* South-East Asia, Far East

THE ARMED FORCES

ROYAL NAVY

Refer to the Royal Navy (caps), thereafter the Navy (retain the cap); *naval* is l/c except in titles such as Royal Naval Volunteer Reserve (RNVR) etc.

Ships are styled *HMS Achilles* or the *Achilles*. They should generally be treated as feminine; thus *she* and *her* rather than *it* and *its*. Ships are named, not christened. Note that Royal Fleet Auxiliary ships are entitled RFA, eg, *RFA Fort George* (not HMS ...)

GENERAL TERMS

alter (not change) **course**

Armed Forces, Armed Services, the Services (caps), but l/c **serviceman, servicewoman**. Also cap **Service** and **Forces** when used adjectivally as in *a Service family*

astern (never behind or following), eg, the *Achilles* was astern of the *Ajax*

Britannia, the former Royal Yacht

company in the Royal Navy, ships do not have crews, they have ship's company

embarked *in*, not *on*

the Fleet (cap)

line ahead, not astern

moored or **made fast**; vessels are never *tied up*

on board is preferable to aboard

pennant, not pendant

ratings, not *other ranks*, in the Navy

Royal Marines (caps)

SBS, the Special Boat Service (no longer Squadron)

serving *in* a warship (but *on* a merchant ship); an officer is *appointed* to serve in *HMS Sheffield*, not posted to serve ... Also note that sailors serve *in a submarine*, even though subs are boats

signalman, not signaller

submarines are called *boats* (not ships) in the Royal Navy

tow the towing ship has the towed ship *in tow*; the towed ship is *under tow*

Union Flag (not Union Jack) in naval contexts, except when flown at the jackstaff

under way

weigh anchor (not *ship anchor*, which would mean that a ship had left her anchor at the bottom of the sea)

RANKS

a. Prefer not to abbreviate ranks in text of news stories; however, in lists of promotions etc on the Court Page, the following abbreviations will apply: Adm, Cdre (Commodore), Capt, Cdr (Commander), Lt-Cdr, Lt, CPO (Chief Petty Officer), L/S (Leading Seaman).

b. *Times* style is to hyphenate those ranks consisting of a compound of two individual designations, eg, Lieutenant-Commander, Commandant-General, Surgeon-Captain; also any rank with vice or rear, eg, Vice-Admiral, Rear-Admiral. We should also hyphenate Commander-in-Chief

c. A flag officer is a rear-admiral or above, exercising command and authorised by the Admiralty to fly a flag. The following are flag ranks: Admiral of the Fleet, Admiral, Vice-Admiral, Rear-Admiral. Although the Duke of Edinburgh is an Admiral of the Fleet, the Fleet is actually commanded by an admiral whose job title is Commander-in-Chief Fleet (CinC Fleet)

THE ARMY

The Army is capped when referred to as the Service, eg, "Two hundred new tanks were bought by the Army yesterday", or "He denied that he hated the Army"; but l/c when used adjectivally, eg, "An army raid was launched yesterday on the front line ...", or "An army spokesman rejected the suggestion ..."

Give soldiers their full title at first mention, eg, General Herbert Carruthers, thereafter General Carruthers or the general. Never refer to them as Mr in news stories.

GENERAL TERMS

beating retreat (not beating the retreat)

guards of honour are ceremonial troops used to greet visiting dignitaries; like all guards, they **are mounted**, as **sentries are posted**

The King's Own Royal Border Regiment (full title)

King's Troop, RHA, remains thus even though the Sovereign is the Queen

Last Post (not *the*) is **sounded**, not played

parade troops march through the streets; they do not parade

Royal Corps of Signals may be contracted to Royal Signals (not RCS)

Royal Engineers can be abbreviated to RE (not REs)

Royal Electrical and Mechanical Engineers (REME for short, never Reme)

The Royal Welch Fusiliers, but **Welsh Guards**

SAS, the Special Air Service (regiment). See SBS under Royal Navy

Trooping the Colour (not Trooping *of* the Colour)

trumpeters, **buglers** cavalry regiments have trumpeters, infantry regiments have buglers. They are not interchangeable

RANKS AND REGIMENTS

One of the trickiest areas is when to include *The* as part of the name of regiments. The answer is *always* to check with an up-to-date *Army List*; with defence cuts and the amalgamation of regiments in the past few years, titles have changed rapidly, so checking is imperative. General styles as follows:

Companies: A Company, B Battery, 94 (Locating) Battery, C Squadron

Battalions: 1st, 2nd etc, and 1st/5th, 6l Field Regiment, RA

Brigades: 24 Infantry Brigade, 5 Airborne Brigade

Divisions: 7th Armoured Division

Corps: X Corps, XII Corps

Armies: First Army

Army Groups: 21 Army Group

With ranks, the same guidance on abbreviation and hyphenation applies as to the Royal Navy (*see* previous section):

a. Prefer not to abbreviate ranks in text of news stories; however, in lists of promotions etc on the Court Page, the following abbreviations will apply; Gen; Lt-Gen; Maj-Gen; Brig; Col; Lt-Col; Maj; Capt; Lt; 2nd Lt; WO1 (Warrant Officer Class 1); WO2; S Sgt (Staff Sergeant); Sgt; Cpl;

Bdr (Bombardier); L Cpl; Pte (Private); Gdsmn (Guardsman); Gnr (Gunner); Rfn (Rifleman)

b. Hyphenate those ranks consisting of a compound of two individual designations, eg, Major-General, Lieutenant-General, Lieutenant-Colonel, Sergeant-Major etc, but not compounds such as Staff Sergeant, Lance Corporal. (Note that Brigadier-General does not exist in the British Army, though it does, eg, in the American and French.)

c. Chief of Defence Staff: a naval Chief of Defence Staff becomes Admiral Sir John Jones; an army one is General Sir John Jones; and an air force one is Air Chief Marshal Sir John Jones, in each case followed by Chief of Defence Staff

d. A field marshal would be either a peer or a knight, so after first mention of, eg, Field Marshal Sir Richard Potts, he would be called Sir Richard

e. Similarly, an officer with a personal title should be described in full at first mention, eg, Lieutenant-General Sir Amos Burke, later Sir Amos or General Burke

ROYAL AIR FORCE

a. Use the Royal Air Force or the RAF in text, not the Air Force (*see* air force in general alphabetical section)

b. With ranks, the same guidance on abbreviation applies as to the Royal Navy and the Army (*see* previous pages); the only RAF rank to take a hyphen is Air Vice-Marshal

c. Abbreviations (in lists only, as above) as follows: AVM (Air Vice-Marshal); Air Cdre (Air Commodore); Gp Capt (Group Captain); Wg Cdr (Wing Commander); Sqn Ldr (Squadron Leader); Flt Lt (Flight Lieutenant); FO (Flying Officer); PO (Pilot Officer); FS (Flight Sergeant); Chief Tech (Chief Technician); Sgt (Sergeant); Cpl (Corporal); SAC/SACW (Senior Aircraftman/Senior Aircraftwoman) etc. NB. *Never* shorten Flight Lieutenant to Lieutenant at subsequent mentions

d. Types of aircraft (not planes): Harrier jump-jet, Tornado (Tornados plural), B52, F111 (no hyphens), etc

e. **RAF crews** went on **operations** (or ops) in the Second World War; American (USAF) crews went on **missions**. Do not confuse

f. RAF Regiment is a Corps within the Royal Air Force

THE ARTS

ART

Titles of paintings, drawings, sculptures and exhibitions are *all* in italic.

DANCE

ballets: titles in italics
cha-cha-cha (not cha-cha)
Latin dancing (cap "L")
pas de deux, corps de ballet: roman
paso doble (two words)
pointe shoes: not point

FILM

film titles take italics
film-maker (hyphen)
film noir (roman)
cinéma-vérité (roman)
auteur (roman)
Palme d'or (roman)
8mm film, 16mm etc
3-D

LITERATURE

All book titles (literature or otherwise) take italics; these include novels, plays, short stories, all poems (short or long), magazine articles, chapter headings etc, as well as textbooks, reference books, biographies etc. But do not italicise the Bible, the Talmud, the Koran, Book of Genesis etc.

MUSIC

Song titles (classical or pop) take italics; no need to cap every word in the title, eg, *Bring it on Home to Me* rather than *Bring It On Home To Me*

Album titles take italics

Opus: Op (Op 28)

Number: No (as in Symphony No 3)

Symphony No 3 (roman caps); but where symphonies have numbers and popular alternative titles (Eroica, Pastoral) the titles, when used, are in italics, eg, *Eroica*. Spell out ordinals, as Mahler's Fourth Symphony (but Symphony No 4)

First Violin Concerto (roman caps, because it is a genre)

Requiem (roman caps, because it is a genre)

Operas: titles take italics, as do arias

Orchestral works with non-genre titles take italics (*Night on the Bare Mountain*)

Mozart works: K527 etc (numbering system of Köchel)

the Proms (no need to spell out Promenade Concerts); Promenaders; the Last Night of the Proms (caps)

tempos (not tempi)

virtuosos (not virtuosi)

THEATRE

Play titles take italics

dramatis personae (roman)

Wyndham's Theatre, London

Act I, scene 2 etc (ie, cap Act and use Roman numeral, l/c scene and Arabic numeral)

TV AND RADIO

Television and radio programmes take italics, except for first mention in reviews, when they go in bold

GENERAL ARTS STYLES

a cappella

Albert Hall, **Festival Hall**, **National Theatre**, generally omit *Royal*; but **Royal Opera House**, **Royal Shakespeare Company**, **Royal Ballet** (which is different from the **Birmingham Royal Ballet**), etc

Arts Council, thereafter the council (l/c) provided the context is clear

arts awards initial cap for titles of awards such as Best Actress, Best Film, Play of the Year etc

Bartók, Béla

the Beatles, the Rolling Stones etc: no need to cap *the* unless at the start of a sentence; but prefer to keep cap "T" with The Who and The The

cinemagoer, dancegoer, theatregoer (each one word)

commedia dell'arte

debut, decor, matinee, premiere: *no* accents

Dvorák, Antonin

hi-fi

Holmes à Court, Janet

Janácek, Leos

mezzo-soprano (hyphen)

nightclub

3-D

subplot, subtext, subtitle

Symphony Hall, Birmingham (omit *the*)

Tate Modern, Tate Britain, Tate Liverpool and **Tate St Ives** (all omit *the*)

ASH caps for abbreviation of Action on Smoking and Health, the anti-smoking pressure group

Ashcroft, Lord (not "of Belize" or of anything else)

Asia-Pacific Economic Co-operation forum (Apec as abbreviation)

assassin to be used only in the murder of a statesman or politician from a political motive (same applies to assassination); not to be used for the killing of general celebrities or others. *See* execution and killer

Assisted Places Scheme (caps), but assisted places (in schools)

assizes, like quarter sessions, no longer function, having been replaced by the Crown Court. *See* quarter sessions

Association of First Division Civil Servants, or First Division Association (FDA) for short

assure you **assure** your life; **ensure** means to make certain; you **insure** against risk

asylum-seekers (hyphenate)

at the present time, at this time use *now*; but avoid the phrase *as of now*

Athenaeum, the. *See* London clubs

Atlantic (Ocean), North Atlantic, South Atlantic, but **transatlantic**

Atomic Energy Authority in the UK (not *Agency*), abbreviated to AEA; but note **International Atomic Energy Agency**, abbreviated to IAEA

ATS short for Auxiliary Territorial Service (not Auxiliary Training Service)

Attorney-General, Solicitor-General (both are hyphenated); they are law officers, not legal officers. *See* Courts special section (page 47)

Auditor-General (with hyphen)

Auntie (not aunty) as colloquialism for the BBC. *See* BBC

Autocue (cap, proprietary)

Autumn Statement (caps). *See* Budget

Awol, absent without leave, not AWOL

AXA (not Axa), the financial services group

axeing (with midde "e"); but try to avoid in sense of cutting jobs, dismissal etc

ay (yes), **aye** (ever), **Ayes** (debate)

Ayckbourn, (Sir) Alan

B

BAA is now the name of the airports operator; it is no longer the British Airports Authority

Baath party, not Ba'ath

Baby Bonds registered as a friendly society trademark, so must not be used in a generic sense or as vernacular for **Child Trust Fund** (initial caps)

baby-boomer

Babygro (cap, proprietary)

baby-walker

baccalaureate use Anglicised spelling with l/c for general use, but cap in specific context of the International Baccalaureate; and note the specifically French examination or degree, the **Baccalauréat** (italic, cap, accent, no final "e")

Bacharach, Burt

backache, **backbreaking**, but **back pain**

BAE Systems, no longer British Aerospace or BAe

B&B with caps and closed up around ampersand as abbreviation for bed and breakfast

back benches (parliamentary) two words; but **backbenchers**, **backbench** (adjectival, as in

backbench revolt). *See* Politics special section (page 131)

back burner (no hyphen), but be sparing of the cliché "on the back burner"

backlash overworked word; always try to avoid

backstreet(s) noun or adjective, no hyphen; similarly, **backyard**

"back to basics" (quotes, no hyphen)

back-up (noun, hyphenate)

bacteria and viruses are different and the terms are not interchangeable. Make sure the terminology is correct. Note that antibiotics are used to treat bacterial but not viral infections. *See* medical terms, meningitis

Bafta (not BAFTA), the British Academy of Film and Television Arts

bail out (as in to bail someone out of trouble; also bail water from a boat); but bale out of an aircraft by parachute, to escape. NB, **bailout** (one word, as noun)

balk not baulk

ball plural in Court Page headlines is *Dances*

ballgown (one word)

balloted, like benefited, budgeted etc, has only one "t"

Balpa British Air Line Pilots' Association

banister not bannister

Bank Holiday, Bank Holiday Monday etc

Bank for International Settlements (not "of")

bankruptcy in Britain people file a petition for bankruptcy; they do not file for bankruptcy

Bar, the (legal); also cap for the Bar of the House of Commons and cap in military honours sense, eg, DFC and Bar. *See* Courts special section (page 47) and Politics special section (page 131)

barbecue, barbecuing

bar mitzvah (l/c, roman); also **bat mitzvah** for girls

Bar school l/c "s", as this is not its official title, and no longer Bar law school. Its full name is the Inns of Court School of Law

Barnardo's, and no longer Dr Barnardo's Homes

barony pertains to barons (eg, Lord X); **baronetcy** to baronets (hereditary titles carrying the prefix Sir, eg, Sir Fred Y; *The Times* does not usually use the Bt suffix). Note, knighthoods are not hereditary although they also use the title Sir. *See* Titles special section (page 171)

Bart's abbreviation of St Bartholomew's Hospital, London

Basle (Switzerland), not Basel. *See* Berne

basically greatly overworked word that rarely adds anything to a sentence. Always try to avoid

basis "on a ... basis" is a cliché and should be avoided; for "employment on a part-time basis" say "part-time employment"

Basque Country (initial caps). *See* Eta

battalion (never batallion). Say the 1st Battalion, the 7th Battalion etc (not First, Seventh). *See* Armed Forces special section (page 14)

Battersea Dogs' Home (formal title is The Dogs' Home, Battersea, but not usually necessary to spell it out)

battle avoid using as a transitive verb as in "The students battled the police ..."; use "fought" or "battled against" instead

BBC no need to spell out as British Broadcasting Corporation, though "the corporation" is a useful alternative in text. Note that the BBC in spring 2002 rebranded its TV channels as BBC One, BBC Two, BBC Three and BBC Four etc (no longer BBC1, BBC2 etc); however, the numeral can still be used in headlines where space is tight. But Radio 1, 2, 3, 4, Radio 5

Live etc keep the numerals. Note BBC Television and BBC Radio (caps). Note also Chairman of the (Board of) Governors takes caps (although chairman in most other cases is l/c). This is because we cap the Director-General and when both appear in the same story it is anomalous to cap the one and not the other. Cap the BBC Board of Governors, but l/c the governors at other mentions. *See* radio, television

BBC Charter (cap when in full, then the charter l/c)

BC. *See* AD

be-all and end-all note hyphens

Beatles, the, no need to cap the unless at the start of a sentence; similarly the Rolling Stones and the Manic Street Preachers etc, but prefer to keep cap "T" with The Who and The The

Beatrix (not Beatrice), Queen of the Netherlands. *See* Holland, Netherlands

Becket St Thomas à Becket (with the à)

Beduin is plural. The singular is Bedu

Beethoven, Ludwig van (not von); normally Beethoven will suffice. *See* Van

beg the question do not confuse with "ask the question". To beg a question is to evade it

Beijing (no longer Peking). *See* Chinese names

Belarus (no longer Belorussia); its people are Belarussians (prefer to Belarusians)

beleaguered rapidly becoming a cliché, especially in a political context, so best avoided

Belfast, North, South, East and West. *See* Ireland

bellringer, **bellringing**, **belltower** (no hyphens). *See* peal

bellwether (not bellweather)

benchmark (no hyphen)

benefited

benzene is a substance obtained from coal-tar; **benzine** is a spirit obtained from petroleum

-berg, **-burg** always check spelling of towns with these endings, and those ending in -burgh, -borough, -brough

Berkeley Square, in the West End of London; similarly, **Berkeley, California**

Bermudian, not Bermudan; but a Bermuda-rigged boat

Berne (Switzerland), not Bern

berserk, not beserk

Berwick-upon-Tweed (the northernmost town in England)

BEST Investment has changed its name again; it is now **Bestinvest**

bestseller (one word); likewise **bestselling**

bête noire, italic and final "e" on noire

Betjeman, Sir John (not Betjamin)

Bevan, Aneurin; **Bevin, Ernest**

Beverly Hills

Bhutto, Benazir; call her Miss rather than Ms or Mrs at subsequent mentions

bi- take care with this difficult prefix. Its correct use is in Latin compounds, where it has the force of two, not half, such as bicentenary/ bicentennial (a two-hundredth anniversary), or biennial (recurring every two years). Biannual means twice a year; to avoid confusion, write out *twice a year*

biased

Bible (cap and roman, not italic), but biblical (l/c); **biblical references** thus – II Corinthians ii, 2; Luke iv, 5. *See* Churches special section (page 37)

Bible Belt (both cap "B")

bid do not use in text as synonym of *effort*, *attempt* or *try*, though it may be used sparingly in headlines in this context

bight is a curve in a coastline or river; **bite** involves teeth. Do not confuse. *See* bite, German Bight

Bill and **Act** caps whether fully identified or not

Bill of Rights cap even when non-specific (eg, "If the Government were to introduce a Bill of Rights …")

billion one thousand million, not a million million. Write £5 billion, £15 billion (£5bn, £15bn in headlines), three billion, 15 billion etc. *See* millions, trillion

Billy Elliot (hit film), not Elliott; but *see* Eliot, T. S.

bin Laden, Osama note l/c "bin", except where it is the first word of a headline or sentence. Avoid the "Mr" designation, as with Saddam Hussein etc. Bin Laden's organisation is **al-Qaeda** (not Qaida). *See* War on Terror

bin-liner (use hyphen)

biological terms. *See* scientific names, with particular reference to Latin terms – cap letter for first (genus) word, then l/c for the second (species); and italicise for all but the most common

Biro is a trade name, so cap; the alternative is *ballpoint pen*

birthday people and animals have birthdays; everything else has anniversaries. Write 33rd birthday, 65th birthday etc (any number higher than **tenth**). *See* numbers

birthrate, **birthright**, **birthplace** (no hyphens), but **birth control**, **birth certificate** etc

Birtwistle, Sir Harrison (composer), not Birtwhistle

bisexual pronouns *he* and *his* can no longer refer to both sexes equally; *he or she* will sometimes do. Always be sensitive in this contentious area

bishops. *See* archbishops

Bishopsgate in the City of London (not Bishopgate)

Bishop's Stortford

bite (as with teeth) must not be confused with the computing term *byte* or the geographical *bight. See* bight, byte, soundbite

blacklist one word as noun or verb. *See* shortlist

blackout (noun, one word)

blacks (people), l/c; do not use "non-whites" and be sensitive to local usage. *African-American* is now often used in the United States, for instance. *See* Coloureds, race

blackspot (accident, unemployment etc), one word; similarly, **troublespot**, **hotspot**

blame take care with this word; blame is attached to causes, not effects. So say "Bad weather is blamed for my bronchitis", *not* "My bronchitis is blamed on bad weather"

bloc use in context such as the former **Soviet bloc**, a **power bloc** etc; but **block vote**

blond for men, **blonde** for women

blood the **National Blood Service** (NBS) – *not* the National Blood Transfusion Service – operates only in England and North Wales. Its parent administrative body is the **National Blood Authority**. The equivalent bodies to the NBS in other countries of the UK are the **Scottish National Blood Transfusion Service**; the **Welsh Blood Service** (for South and Mid Wales, but not for North Wales); and the **Northern Ireland Blood Transfusion Service**

bloodied but unbowed; but **red-blooded** etc

blood sports (two words; similarly field sports). *See* foxhunt

Bloomingdale's

Blue cap both for an Oxbridge sportsman or woman and for the award itself. *See* Sports special section (page 160)

blue-collar workers, as white-collar workers

blueprint avoid this greatly overworked word when all you mean is plan, scheme or proposal

bluffers be very cautious. *The Bluffer's Guide/Guides* are trademarks, rigorously protected by their publishers. So generic phrases such as "a bluffer's guide to …" must be avoided

Blu-Tack proprietary so must cap

bmi british midland (no longer British Midland), the airline; note also easyJet and buzz, but Go (now with cap)

Boadicea not *Boudicca*

boat is generally used of a small vessel, including fishing boats up to the size of a trawler; a ship is a large seagoing vessel big enough to carry smaller boats. In the Royal Navy, submarines are called boats. All take the pronoun *she* and the possessive *her. See* ships

Boat Race   caps for the annual Oxford-Cambridge race

Boche, derogatory slang for Germans; **Bosch**, the household appliance or power tools manufacturer

boffin   do not use as a synonym of *scientist*, except ironically or in direct quotes

Bogart, Humphrey, but **(Sir) Dirk Bogarde**

bogey (golf), **bogie** (wheels), **bogy** (ghost); but note **bogeyman**

Bogotá (capital of Colombia)

Bohemian (cap noun), but bohemian (adj, l/c)

Bolshevik

bombs   car bomb, fire bomb, nail bomb, petrol bomb etc, but hyphenate verbal or adjectival use, eg, to fire-bomb, a nail-bomb attack

bombshell   in metaphorical use, as in "drop a bombshell", a cliché that has no place in *The Times*

bonanza   another greatly overworked word that should be avoided wherever possible

Bonham Carter, Helena (no hyphen)

Bonhams (no apostrophe), the auction house; still known simply as Bonhams despite recent (summer 2002) on-off merger activity

Boodle's, the London club. *See* London clubs

Booth, Cherie   the Prime Minister's wife should be referred to as Cherie Booth wherever possible rather than Cherie Blair. Refer to Cherie Blair only in context where she is clearly in the role of the PM's wife, eg, at summit meetings or on the campaign trail. Do not refer to her as Britain's First Lady. In legal contexts, write Cherie Booth, QC, at first mention; subsequent mentions, Ms Booth

Boothroyd, Baroness (not of Sandwell or anywhere else)

bored with, not *of*

borstals no longer exist; they are now young offender institutions

bortsch (Russian or Polish soup)

Bosphorus

Boutros Boutros Ghali (no hyphens), the former UN Secretary-

General; at subsequent mentions, Dr
Boutros Ghali. His successor is the
Ghanaian **Kofi Annan**

Bowes Lyon no hyphen for most
of the family, but always important
to check in *Who's Who* or *Debrett*.
The late Queen Elizabeth the
Queen Mother did *not* take the
hyphen

bow-tie

box office as noun, two words; but
hyphenate when adjectival (eg, box-
office success)

boyfriend, girlfriend

Boy Scouts are now simply Scouts
in the UK. Cub Scouts have replaced
Wolf Cubs; Scoutleaders have
replaced Scoutmasters. Also cap
Scouting in the context of the
movement. In the US there are still
Boy Scouts. Similarly for Guides,
Girl Guides

Boy's Own as generic phrase, cap
and roman; but the old publication
was called *The Boy's Own Paper*

Braille (now cap)

brainchild try to avoid this cliché

branch (in police context): **Special
Branch, Anti-Terrorist Branch**

Brands Hatch

breakout, breakdown (as noun,
each one word); but to *break out* etc,
and **break-up** (hyphen)

breast-feed(ing), use hyphen

Breathalyser (cap, proprietary), but
to breathalyse (l/c, generic)

breathtaking (no hyphen)

Brent Spar is *not* an oil platform,
still less a rig. It is a **storage buoy**
and must be referred to in no other
way. Note that **oil platforms** stand
on the seabed; **oilrigs** are small
mobile installations for oil
exploration

Bretton Woods (as in world trade)

Breughel (the painters)

bridges cap as in Severn Bridge,
London Bridge, Southwark Bridge,
Golden Gate Bridge

Bridget Jones's Diary (not *Jones'*),
novel and film

Bridgwater (Somerset) has no
middle "e"

Brink's-Mat

Britain or **Great Britain** =
England, Wales and Scotland.
United Kingdom = Britain and
Northern Ireland. **British Isles** =
United Kingdom and the Republic
of Ireland, Isle of Man and Channel
Islands. Take every care with these
distinctions

Britannia. *See* Royal Yacht

British Athletic Federation (not
Athletics)

British Home Stores has changed
its abbreviation to **Bhs**

British Social Attitudes Survey, 2001; dates of the survey vary, but use preceding comma whenever

British Standards Institution (BSI), not Institute. It awards companies, goods etc its Kitemark (cap)

Britpop (not Brit Pop), but **Brit Art** (two words)

Brittany (Bretagne in French)

Broadcasting Standards Commission, which merged the Broadcasting Standards Council and Broadcasting Complaints Commission, is now (2002) being incorporated into the Office of Communications (Ofcom). *See* regulators

Broadmoor inmates are patients, not prisoners

broadsheet is better than *quality* in describing the serious British press

Brooke, Lord Justice (not Brook), the Court of Appeal judge

Brookings Institution (in Washington), not *Institute*

Brooks's, the London club. *See* London clubs

brownfield, **greenfield** (as in building sites). But note green belt (two words)

Brummie (not Brummy), **Geordie**, **Scouse** etc, people and dialect, all capped. *See* Cockney

Brylcreem

BSE bovine spongiform encephalopathy, or "mad cow" disease

BSkyB The News Corporation, parent company of *The Times*, owns 36.3 per cent of BSkyB (British Sky Broadcasting Group Ltd). So use the formula: BSkyB, in which The News Corporation, parent company of *The Times*, has a 36.3 per cent stake … BSkyB can also be called an associate company of News International, or of News Corp. There is a choice of up to 40 channels available in the UK on the Astra satellite; BSkyB wholly owns 11. *See* News International, *The Times*

BT is the usual abbreviated form of British Telecommunications plc, but it is often convenient to call the company British Telecom at first mention, and BT subsequently

Budget cap the British Budget, otherwise l/c. Note Budget day (l/c "d"); also note **Pre-Budget Report** and **Autumn Statement** (caps)

budgeting

Buffett, Warren, American investment banker

Buggins's turn (not Buggins')

builder's merchant(s)

building societies cap when we give the full name, eg, Skipton

Building Society, thereafter the Skipton, or the society etc. Take care with societies that have become banks. *See* Abbey National

Bulger, James (not Jamie)

bullion is gold or silver in unminted form

bull-mastiff, bull-terrier. *See* dogs

bullring, bullfight(er). Note that the old Bull Ring Centre in Birmingham is being redeveloped and will be known as **Bullring**

bull's-eye

bungee jumping (no hyphen)

BUPA, not Bupa

burka prefer to burqa

Burma, not Myanmar (except in direct quotes); the inhabitants are Burmese, while Burmans are a Burmese people

Burnet, Sir Alastair

Burns Night (caps, no apostrophe) falls on January 25

burnt, not burned

Burton upon Trent (no hyphens); and note the colloquial **gone for a burton** (l/c)

bus, buses (noun); but in verbal use, **busses, bussed, bussing**

Bush, George W. do not use Jr.

President Bush at first mention, then Mr Bush or the President. Refer to his father as the first President Bush or George Bush Sr

Bushey, Hertfordshire; **Bushy Park**, near Hampton Court

Bussell, Darcey (the ballerina)

but for use at start of a sentence, *see* punctuation

Butlins holiday camps (no apostrophe); now known as resorts

buyout and **buyback** (one word); but prefer **buy-in, take-off, shake-out, shake-up, sell-off, sell-out** etc with hyphens, wherever the composite looks hideous

buzz, the no-frills airline, and note easyJet and Go

buzzword (one word)

by-election

bylaw

bypass (noun or verb)

by-product

bystander

byte is a computer term for a small collection of bits (binary digits), roughly equivalent to one character. Do not confuse with *bite* (as with teeth). But note **soundbite**

Byzantine (cap in all contexts)

C

cabbie (not cabby) as colloquialism for taxi driver

Cabinet cap in both British and foreign use, whether used as a noun or adjectivally. The only exception is the informal "kitchen cabinet". Note Cabinet Office, Cabinet Secretary (or Secretary of the Cabinet). Cabinet committees should be capped, eg, the Cabinet Committee on Science and Technology. *See* Politics special section (page 131)

Caernarfon (town and parliamentary constituency, no longer Caernarvon), but Lord Carnarvon

Caesarean section

café (with accent)

caffeine; prefer to caffein

cagoule, but **kaftan**

call-up (noun), to call up

camaraderie (not cameraderie)

Camborne, Cornwall (not Cambourne)

Cambridge University colleges and halls are:
Christ's College; Churchill College; Clare College; Clare Hall; Corpus Christi College; Darwin College; Downing College; Emmanuel College; Fitzwilliam College; Girton College; Gonville and Caius College; Homerton College; Hughes Hall; Jesus College; King's College; Lucy Cavendish College; Magdalene College; New Hall; Newnham College; Pembroke College; Peterhouse; Queens' College; Robinson College; St Catharine's College; St Edmund's College; St John's College; Selwyn College; Sidney Sussex College; Trinity College; Trinity Hall; Wolfson College

camellia (not camelia)

Cammell Laird, the Birkenhead shipyard (not Liverpool)

Campbell, Alastair (not Alistair), Tony Blair's communications and strategy director

Camp X-Ray (note caps) at Guantanamo Bay (no accent) in Cuba; *see* War on Terror, X-ray

Camra, the Campaign for Real Ale

canal boats do not use the term "barge" indiscriminately; **barges** are towed, unpowered boats for transporting cargo. Use the term **narrowboats** for the boats on the narrow 7ft-wide canals, or **canal boats** for wider vessels on wider canals. If in doubt, use canal boat (never canal barge)

CanalPlus, the French TV channel (avoid the canal+ logo style)

cancer take care not to describe cancer as "the biggest killer" in the UK. Heart disease is

cannon (military, same form for singular and plural); but **canons** (ecclesiastical, both churchmen and church laws), and **canon** as a collection/list of an author

canvas (material, painting); **canvass** (votes)

Canton, now Guangzhou. *See* Chinese names

CAP now cap Common Agricultural Policy; similarly, Common Fisheries Policy (CFP)

Cape Town

capitalisation in general, the proper names of people and places, formal titles or titles of important offices, and the names of well-known and substantial institutions, all require capitals. As a rule of thumb, **cap specifics** (eg, the French Foreign Minister), but **l/c non-specifics** (eg, EU foreign ministers). But some terms, eg, **Act**, **Bill**, **Cabinet**, **Civil Service**, always cap. *See* initials

capsize. *See* -ise, -isation

captions when space is tight, especially on single-column "mug

shots", the name should be just the surname, even when the person is titled, eg, Sir Marcus Fox would be simply Fox, as in headlines. Where women are photographed, be sensitive – readers complain endlessly about our omitting the Christian name, especially in court cases where the woman is the victim. Where possible, give the woman's first name, though this is not a hard and fast ruling.

When identifying faces with *left* and *right* etc, use commas rather than brackets (eg, Fred Smith, left, and his wife leaving the court); make the identification in the caption fit the sequence of faces (left to right) in the photograph

car boot sale (no hyphen)

carcass

cardholder

Carlos the Jackal (no quotes, no commas); always mention his full name, Ilich Ramírez Sánchez, somewhere in the story

carmaker (one word)

car park (two words), **multistorey car park**

carpetbagger (one word)

Carrott, Jasper (not Carrot)

carry out do not use as synonym of *do*

cashcard (in general sense), **cashflow**, **cashback**

Cashpoint is Lloyds TSB Bank's cash machine system, so takes the cap and should not be used generically; in the general sense, use cash dispenser or cash machine, or less formally, hole in the wall

Castro, President (Fidel) no longer call him Dr after first mention, but Señor or the President

catapult (not catapault)

Catch-22 avoid the grossly overworked cliché *Catch-22 situation*

cathedrals cap when giving the full name, eg, St Paul's Cathedral, Wells Cathedral; similarly the names of churches, eg, St Mary's Church, Ely, unless we know that the church name specifically excludes it, eg, St Stephen's, Ely

Catherine always check the spelling. A Catherine wheel (firework); St Catharine's College, Cambridge; St Katharine Docks, London

Catholic in church context, say Roman Catholic at first mention, then Catholic. *See* Churches special section (page 37)

Catmark, the new financial products version of the Kitemark; similarly, Cat standard etc

cat's eyes should preferably be called reflecting roadstuds. Catseye is a trademark

caviar no final "e"

CBI do not spell out as Confederation of British Industry

CD-Rom (compact disc, read only memory); **CD-i** (the interactive compact disc system)

ceasefire

Ceausescu, Nicolae (not Ceaucescu)

ceilidh social gathering (Highland)

Cellophane is proprietary, so cap

celsius, centigrade use either term. In news stories, use centigrade first, then fahrenheit in brackets at first mention, eg, "The temperature rose to 16C (61F)". *See* metric

Census cap in specific cases, such as the 1901 Census, the 2001 Census, but l/c generally and adjectivally

centenarian, and *see also* **septuagenarian**, **octogenarian**, **nonagenarian**

centenaries use centenary, bicentenary, tercentenary; after that, say four (five) hundredth anniversary

Center Parcs

Central Europe (with cap C)

Central St Martins College of Art and Design (no apostrophe), St Martins at subsequent mentions

Centre, the use the cap in

political context of the Centre, as with Left and Right. Similarly, Centre Left, Centre Right as nouns, but a centre-left politician (l/c adjectival, as with a right-wing policy). *See* Left, Right, Politics special section (page 131)

Centre Court. *See* Wimbledon

centrepiece (no hyphen)

centring, but centering of arches in bridge-building

centuries the style is the 3rd century BC, the 9th century, the 18th century etc; and adjectivally with the hyphen, eg, 20th-century architecture

CERN (all caps), the European Organisation for Nuclear Research, based in Geneva

Ceylon now **Sri Lanka**. The people are Sri Lankan, the majority group are the Sinhalese

cha-cha-cha (not cha-cha)

chainsaw (one word)

chairman is still the common usage referring to men and women, except in quotes, but *chairwoman* is acceptable. Avoid chair and chairperson (except in quotes and phrases such as "addressing remarks to the chair"). In most cases, keep chairman l/c, but occasionally cap, as with BBC, Bar Council, and US Federal Reserve Board

chamber (l/c) of the House of

Commons. *See* Politics special section (page 131)

champagne (l/c) use only for the product of the Champagne region of France; otherwise write, eg, Russian sparkling wine. The champagne producers protect their name rigorously. *See* wines

Champions League (European football), no apostrophe; the later knockout stage of the competition becomes the European Cup

changeable

Changing the Guard (not ... of the Guard). *See* Trooping

Channel 4 (not Four); but the former Channel 5 has been rebranded (September 2002) simply as **Five**. *See* television

Channel Tunnel (with cap T), but thereafter l/c tunnel if the context is clear; also, **Channel Tunnel Rail Link** (now all caps). *See* Eurotunnel

Chanukkah prefer this to variants such as Hanukkah etc, for the Jewish festival of lights

charge that an Americanism, never to be used as a synonym of *allege that*

charisma has become a boring cliché; find an alternative such as *presence, inspiration* etc

Charity Commission (not Charities)

Charollais (cattle or sheep)

charters (as in John Major's initiative). *See* Citizen's, Parent's, Patient's; note **Charter Mark** (two words)

Château Lafite (no hyphen, and not *Lafitte*)

chat room (two words) but **chatline** (one)

chat show, game show, quiz show, talk show etc (no hyphens when used as noun but use the hyphen when adjectival, eg, chat-show host); note also **chatline, sexline**

cheap goods are cheap, prices are low

Chechnya (not Chechenia); adjective **Chechen**

check-in (noun), but **checklist, checkout counter**

cheerleader (one word)

Chekhov, Anton

Cheney, Dick (no longer Richard)

chequebook one word, either as noun or adjective (eg, chequebook journalism)

chess names note **Garry Kasparov, Anatoly Karpov, Judit Polgar**. Note also Fide, not FIDE, and grandmaster (l/c). *See* Russian names

Chester-le-Street

chickenpox (no hyphen; similarly **smallpox**)

Chief Constable caps when referring to a specific, as in Chief Constable of Lancashire; thereafter, the chief constable. *See* police ranks

Chief Inspector of Prisons / ... of Schools; also, **Chief Medical Officer**

Chief Whip (caps). *See also* whips

childcare (as healthcare)

ChildLine, the charity (note cap L)

Children Act of 1989 (not Children's); also, note **The Children's Society** (cap The)

child-sex abusers / offenders (use hyphen)

Child Trust Fund (initial caps). A friendly society has registered Baby Bond as a trademark, so *baby bonds* must not be used in a generic sense or as vernacular

chimpanzees are apes, not monkeys

Chinese names use the Pinyin rather than the traditional Wade-Giles, so write Beijing, Mao Zedong (though Chairman Mao or just Mao are acceptable), Zhou Enlai etc. For Chinese place names, follow spellings in *The Times Atlas of the World*: eg, Guangzhou (formerly Canton), Sichuan (formerly Szechuan). *See* Peking

chocoholic, but **shopaholic** and **workaholic**

chopper and **copter** are never to be used as substitutes for helicopter, even in headlines

Christ Church (the Oxford college), never Christ Church College. *See* Peterhouse; also Oxford

Christchurch, in Dorset and New Zealand

christened people are christened, ships and trains etc are named

Christian, **Christianity**, unchristian, non-Christian, antichristian, Antichrist

Christian Democrat is noun and adjective, as in Christian Democrat MP

Christian names take care in context of non-Christians; in such cases, use *forename* or *first name*

Christian terms cap the Apostles, the Bible, the (Ten) Commandments, the Cross, the Crucifixion, the Disciples, the Resurrection, the Gospels, Mass, Holy Communion (and simply Communion), Eucharist, Blessed Sacrament, Advent, Nativity (but a nativity play, adjectival), the Scriptures; also He and His when referring to God and Jesus Christ. Use l/c for evensong, matins. Note Antichrist. *See* Churches special section (page 37)

Christie's (also Christie's, New York, and now Christie's International, all with apostrophe)

Christmas Day, **Christmas Eve**

Church cap in context of the institution (Anglican, Roman Catholic, Orthodox, whatever), but not adjectivally. *See* archbishops, and Churches special section (page 37)

churchwarden (one word)

cider (not cyder)

CIMA, the Chartered Institute of Management Accountants (all caps, at their insistence)

Cincinnati, Ohio

cinemagoer, as concertgoer, theatregoer etc

CinemaScope is a trade name and must be capped (note also cap "S" in middle)

cipher (not cypher)

circa abbreviate simply as c (roman) followed by a space

cissy, **cissies** (not sissy)

Cites (not CITES), the Convention on International Trade in Endangered Species

Citizens Advice Bureau/ Bureaux no apostrophe, and final "x" as plural

Citizen's Charter

Citroën

City of London, the City, City prices. *See* London

City and Guilds of London Institute (abbreviated to **City & Guilds**, with ampersand)

THE CHURCHES

GENERAL STYLES

1. Use **caps** with, eg, the Church of England, the Roman Catholic Church, the United Reformed Church, the Methodist Church, the Church Army. Also cap the **Church** in context of the institution (but not adjectivally, as in "the vicar accused church authorities yesterday …"). For individual churches, write, eg, St James's Church, Bighampton, or simply St James's, Bighampton.

2. Note that the **Church of Ireland**, the **Church in Wales** (NB *in*) and the **Scottish Episcopal Church** are Anglican but disestablished, while the **Church of Scotland** is Presbyterian but established.

3. The **General Synod**, cap at first mention, thereafter the synod (l/c). It has three Houses: of Bishops, Clergy and Laity.

4. The **Church Commissioners** (cap first mention, then the commissioners l/c) have three chief officers, the First (Second, Third) Church Estates Commissioner.

5. The Queen is **Supreme Governor of the Church of England**, *not* head of the Church of England.

6. Persons of the **Trinity** take the **cap pronoun**, eg, God is He; Jesus's teachings, His example.

7. Use the cap for the **Bible** (but not for biblical), the **Apostles**, the **(Ten) Commandments**, the **Cross**, the **Crucifixion**, the **Resurrection**, the **Disciples**, the **Gospels**, the **Scriptures**, **Holy Scripture**, **(Requiem) Mass**, **(Holy) Communion**, **Eucharist**, **Blessed Sacrament** etc.

8. Use l/c for **ordination**, **baptism**, **confirmation**, **last rites**, **psalms** (but the Book of Psalms). Also l/c **matins**, **evensong**.

9. Always say **Roman Catholic** at first mention; thereafter Catholic is acceptable.

10. **The Pope**: not usually necessary to give his full name, eg, Pope John Paul II (unless several Popes are mentioned in a story), but always cap. Note **papacy**, **pontiff** (l/c).

11. Use cap for **Nonconformist** and **Free Churches**. Note that the **United Reformed Church** is composed of the former

Congregational Church and the Presbyterian Church of England; but some "Congregational" congregations remain outside the reformed group.

12. In **Scotland**, distinguish the **Free Church of Scotland** (the "Wee Frees") from the established **Church of Scotland** and also from the **Presbyterian Church of Scotland**. Note the Moderator of the General Assembly of the Church of Scotland (not Moderator of the Church of Scotland).

13. Never ever write the Rev Brown or (even worse) Rev Brown. This would be among the worst solecisms for *The Times* to commit. The correct style is **the Rev Joseph Brown**, thereafter Mr Brown.

14. The **Archbishop of Canterbury** is Primate of All England; the **Archbishop of York** is Primate of England.

15. **Anglican bishops** are consecrated, **Roman Catholic bishops** ordained.

16. In the United States, Scotland and elsewhere, **Episcopal(ian)** means Anglican.

17. **churchgoer** (one word).

18. **Vicar** must not be used as a generic word for priest, parson, clergyman etc. Vicar means specifically the incumbent of a parish (unless a rector). If in doubt, *clergyman* is usually a safer term.

19. Names of **hymns** go in italics.

20. **Biblical references** are written thus: II Corinthians ii, 2; Luke iv, 5.

21. The **Bible** is always cap and roman, but **biblical** is l/c. **Books of the Bible** also caps and roman, eg, Book of Job, as is the **Koran**, the **Talmud**.

22. Cap **Diocese** in specifics, such as the Diocese of Chichester, Guildford Diocese, but l/c in general use, and l/c **diocesan**

23. **evangelical(s)** keep l/c in general church contexts except when part of an official title such as the Evangelical Alliance

TITLES

1. **Senior clergy, Anglicans**: by convention, the names of **bishops and archbishops** always follow the title of their office, eg, the Archbishop of Canterbury, Dr George Carey; the Archbishop of Barchester, the

Most Rev John Smith; or (for diocesan bishops), the Bishop of Barchester, the Right Rev John Smith. Use Dr when appropriate, though not all high ecclesiastics have doctorates; eg, the Bishop of Lowchester, Dr John Smith; subsequent references, the Archbishop (Bishop), or Dr Smith (if so entitled) – never Mr Smith.

Below archbishops and bishops, similar styles prevail: for **archdeacons**, the Archdeacon of Barchester, the Ven John Smith (thereafter Mr Smith, or, more commonly, Canon Smith); for **cathedral deans and provosts**, the Dean of Barchester, the Very Rev John Smith (Dean Smith); **rural deans** are just the Rev John Smith (Mr Smith); **canons and prebendaries** are Canon/Prebendary John Smith, thereafter Canon Smith.

2. **Senior clergy, Roman Catholic: archbishops**, at first mention, the Roman Catholic Archbishop of Liverpool, the Most Rev Patrick Kelly; subsequent mentions Archbishop Kelly or the Archbishop; **bishops**, first mention the Roman Catholic Bishop of Plymouth, the Right Rev Christopher Budd, thereafter Bishop Budd or the Bishop; very few Catholic archbishops or bishops have doctorates, but if we are sure a certain one has, he can be called Dr Budd.

The Archbishop of Westminster, Cardinal X: no need to say Roman Catholic Archbishop of Westminster, but note Roman Catholic Archdiocese of Westminster. Subsequent mentions, Cardinal X or the Cardinal.

Monsignor (Mgr abbreviated) can now be used for Roman Catholic archbishops or bishops in Britain (where appropriate), as well as in foreign contexts.

3. **Junior clergy**: Christian priests, **deacons, ministers, rectors, vicars of all denominations except Roman Catholic or Orthodox** should be, eg, the Rev Frank Faith at first mention, thereafter Mr Faith (see General Styles, para 13). For **women clergy**, write the Rev Joan Faith, thereafter Mrs Faith or Miss Faith.

Roman Catholic and Orthodox clergy should be Father Justin Hope at first mention (avoid the ugly Fr abbreviation), thereafter Father Hope (Catholic), but Father Justin (Orthodox). Also use Father with Benedictines, eg, Father Goode, not Dom Goode.

For **nuns**, use Sister Charity, Mother Charity, Mother Teresa.

Jesuits take designation SJ on first mention, eg, "the Rev Albert Leader, SJ, said yesterday …"

4. **Foreign prelates**: in Ireland, Africa, North America etc, say Anglican Bishop of . . ., Roman Catholic Bishop of . . .; but in countries where, for example, Roman Catholicism is the overwhelming faith, the denomination may be superfluous (eg, the Archbishop of Warsaw …) or supplied by context.

5. In **South Africa**, the Anglican Church is called the Church of the Province of Southern Africa (or Church of the Province, or the Anglican Church). The Church of England is a separate entity, which split from the Anglican Communion in the late 19th century. The Church of the Province has a more Roman Catholic or High Church flavour than most Anglican churches in England, as seen in the dress of bishops, wider use of incense and Stations of the Cross in churches, etc.

Civil Guard(s) (Spanish police), use initial caps

Civil List (caps)

Civil Service, but **civil servants**. Always cap Civil Service, even in adjectival use, eg, a Civil Service memorandum. Caps to be restored to the administrative grade, ie, Permanent Secretary, Deputy Secretary and Assistant Secretary; thus, Sir Alfred Beach, Permanent Secretary to the Ministry of Defence. For executive grade (ie, below Assistant Secretary), use l/c. Note also Secretary of the Cabinet and Head of the Home Civil Service. *See* Politics special section (page 131)

claim do not use when simply *said* or *declared* would do. The word carries a suspicion of incredulity. Also, avoid the loose construction in sentences such as "The firm launched a drink which is claimed to promote learning ability". This should read ". . . a drink which, it is claimed, promotes learning ability"

clamour, **clamouring** but **clamorous**

clampdown not banned, but use as little as possible

Claridge's

Class A, B or C drugs (cap C)

Clause Four (as in Labour Party policy); but Clause 4 permissible in headlines

clichés have no place in *The Times*. Some of the most common, to be resisted strongly in almost every context, are: **backlash**, **basically**, **beleaguered**, **blueprint**,

bombshell, **bonanza**, **brainchild**, **chaos**, **charisma**, **clampdown**, **consensus**, **crackdown**, **crisis**, **crunch**, **drama/dramatic**, **escalate**, **facelift**, **gunned down**, **hopefully**, **ironically**, **legendary**, **major**, **massive**, **mega-**, **nightmare**, **prestigious**, **quantum leap**, **reportedly**, **shambles**, **shock**, **shoot-out**, **situation**, **trauma/traumatic**, **unique**

climate change levy (l/c)

clingfilm (l/c, one word)

closed-circuit television

clothing   say menswear, women's wear, children's wear, sportswear. *See* wear

cloud-cuckoo-land (two hyphens)

clubs. *See* London clubs

co-   the prefix does not normally require a hyphen even before an "e" or another "o" unless confusion might result. Thus **co-operate** (but **uncooperative**), **co-opt**, **co-ordinate** (but **uncoordinated**), **coeducation**, **coexist**. *See* **co-production**

coalface, **coalfield**, **coalmine** (each one word), **coalminer** (but prefer miner). *See* gasfield, oilfield

coastguard   l/c and one word, in the British context; but note the new Coastguard Agency (caps), though the coastguard service

(generic) retains the l/c. Note also the US Coast Guard

coasts   cap South Coast, East Coast and West Coast in British context (as in West Coast Main Line – now all caps); also East Coast and West Coast in US

coats of arms. *See* heraldry

Coca-Cola (hyphen); similarly **Pepsi-Cola**

cockfight (no hyphen), as bullfight and dogfight

Cockney   cap for the person or the dialect, but l/c for general adjectival use, eg, a cockney welcome

coeducation(al), but permissible to use co-ed in headlines as coed would look hideous

coexist

cognoscenti   roman, not italic

Coldstream Guards may be called the Coldstream and the men Coldstreamers or Coldstream Guards; neither should be called Coldstreams. *See* Armed Forces special section (page 14)

Cold War

Coliseum. *See* Colosseum

collarbone (one word)

collectibles (not -ables), items sought by collectors

collective nouns   usually use the singular verb, as with corporate bodies (the company, the Government, the council etc). But this rule is not inviolable: the key is to stick to the singular or plural throughout the story – sentences such as "The committee, which was elected recently, presented their report" are unacceptable

Colombia is the country, while **Columbia** is the Hollywood studio, university, river and Washington district. Also, note **British Columbia** and **Pre-Columbian**

Colosseum in Rome; **Coliseum** in London

Coloureds (in South Africa), cap

Columbia. *See* Colombia

comedienne avoid wherever possible; use comedian for both sexes. *See* feminine designations

comeuppance (no hyphen)

Commander-in-Chief, **Officer Commanding** (caps)

Commandments cap in biblical context, as the Ten Commandments, the Fourth Commandment. *See* Christian terms

commando, plural **commandos** (not -oes)

Commission, **Commissioner**. *See* European

Commissioner of the Metropolitan Police; similarly, cap City of London Police, British Transport Police and all police forces when the full title is given. For full list, *see* police forces

committee note 1922 Committee (cap) of Tory backbenchers. Committees of inquiry etc should be capped only when the full title is given. Cabinet and select committees should be capped. *See* next entry and Cabinet, select committees, Wicks, royal commissions, Conservative, Tory, and Politics special section (page 131)

Committee on Standards in Public Life examines standards of conduct of all holders of public office (can be referred to as the Wicks Committee after Sir Nigel Wicks, its new chairman – no longer Neill or Nolan). It is different from the **Select Committee on Standards and Privileges**, which deals with the conduct of MPs (subsequent mentions, the Privileges Select Committee or l/c the committee). *See* Wicks

Common Agricultural Policy (now caps); similarly, Common Fisheries Policy (CFP). *See* CAP

Common Market usually use EU or EC (*see* Europe), though Common Market is acceptable in its historic context

common sense (noun), but commonsense, commonsensical (adjective)

Common Serjeant. *See* Courts special section (page 47)

Commonwealth Heads of Government Meeting (caps)

communiqué

communism, communist as with socialism and socialist, the best rule-of-thumb is to cap only when in specific party context, eg, a Communist candidate, a Communist rally, the Communist Mayor of Lille; but communist ideology, communist countries etc. It will help to think of a parallel with conservative/conservatism or liberal/liberalism. But Marxist, Stalinist, Nazi and Fascist should be capped

Community Fund new name for the National Lottery Charities Board. *See* Lotto, National Lottery

companies abbreviate to Co in, eg, John Brown & Co. Company is singular. Full points in company titles usually unnecessary, as in W H Smith and J Sainsbury. Do not abbreviate Ford of Europe to Fords, Swan Hunter to Swans etc. *See* Ltd, plc

NB, do not confuse the words *company* and *firm*, even in headlines. A firm implies a business partnership, as in the legal or accountancy professions, estate agents etc

comparatively, relatively avoid using as synonyms of *fairly* or *middling*

compare with/to *compare with* (the more common use) when differences or contrasts are the point

– "compare the saints with the devils" or "compared with last year's figures" etc; *compare to* for likenesses – "compare this image to a damsel fair"

compass points in the UK, regional phrases, if well established and in common use, take caps, as in the **North**, the **South**, the **West**, the **South East**, the **North East**, the **North West**, the **South West**, the **West Country**, the **West Midlands**, the **East Midlands**, **East Anglia, North Wales, South Wales, West Wales**, the **East/West End of London**.

But adjectivally, **southeast England** (though still the **South East of England**).

Overseas, cap the following: the **Midwest** (US), **Central America, West Africa, North Africa, East Africa, Central Africa, South Africa** but **southern Africa, North** and **South Atlantic** and **Pacific**, the **Middle/Far East**, but **sub-Saharan Africa** and **south India** etc

complement (completing something); but **compliment** (praise or tribute); **complimentary**, as in free gifts etc

Comprehensive Spending Review (initial caps)

comprise means to consist of, be composed of; *see* include

Comptroller General

concertgoer (as with partygoer, theatregoer), but concert hall

confectionery (sweets etc; not -ary)

conference keep l/c in Labour Party conference, Lib Dem conference etc

Congo take care to distinguish between the Democratic Republic of Congo (formerly Zaire) and Congo-Brazzaville (formerly French Congo). *See* Zaire

Congress (US), but congressional l/c, and congressman also l/c except when with a name, eg, Congressman John Waldorfburger; but generally try to avoid this construction and say John W, a congressman from Minnesota, etc. *See* Senate

Congress Party in India takes cap "P" and is no longer Congress (I)

conman (one word, as hitman)

connection

Connolly, Billy, the comedian

consensus (never concensus); the word is a cliché that should be avoided wherever possible

Conservative Party, Conservative Central Office – second mention Central Office (never CCO) – but Conservative chairman, manifesto etc; Tory is permissible as a less formal alternative, but note Tory party (l/c "p"). Abbreviate in lists etc to C (not Con). *See* Tory, Politics special section (page 131)

considerable avoid its use as a lazy adjective implying emphasis

Consignia is being renamed (late 2002) as Royal Mail Group, of which the Post Office is a trading subsidiary. *See* Post Office

Consolidated Fund, the

consortium, plural *consortiums* (not consortia); as a general rule, use the *-ums* plural. *See* memorandums etc

constitution of a country is capped only when an actual document, eg, the American Constitution, but the British constitution

consult never say *consult with*

Consumers' Association

Contact Group, the UN group on former Yugoslavia (US, Russia, Britain, France, Italy and Germany) has been replaced by the **Peace Implementation Council**

Continent, the, referring to mainland Europe, but l/c **continental**

continuous means without intermission; **continual** means frequently recurring

contract out has no hyphen

Contras, the (cap in Nicaragua context)

Controller of Radio 1 etc (cap "C"). *See* BBC

controversial delete from 99 stories out of 100

convener, not convenor

convertible (not -able), noun and adjective

conveyor belt; a **conveyer** is a person who conveys

Cooke, Alistair (not Alastair)

cooling towers pictures of these should not be used to illustrate stories about air pollution. They emit water vapour, which is harmless

Co-op the Co-operative Group is the new name (January 2001) for the Co-operative Wholesale Society. The Co-op remains an acceptable abbreviation

co-operate, co-ordinate etc; but uncooperative, uncoordinated, non-cooperation

co-production, co-producer etc (use hyphen to avoid ambiguity with copro-, as in dung)

copycat (no hyphen)

copyright (sole right in artistic work etc); **copywriter** (advertising)

cornflake (generic), but *see* Kellogg's

Coronation cap when referring to a specific event, such as Elizabeth II's in 1953, and also cap Coronation Oath; but l/c in most adjectival uses, eg, coronation ceremony, coronation broadcast

coroner's court at inquests, the coroner is l/c unless specific, as in

the Westminster Coroner. Juries return the verdict, the coroner records it. There are no coroner's inquests in Scotland: violent deaths are reported to the Procurator Fiscal, who may hold an inquiry. *See* Courts special section (page 47)

correspondents wherever possible, write the political correspondent of *The Times*, the Moscow correspondent of *The Times* etc; but the *Times* political correspondent, the *Times* Moscow correspondent etc, is permissible. *See The Times*

cortège (use accent)

coruscating (not corruscating) means sparkling or scintillating, *not* abrasive or corrosive

Côte d'Azur (no final "e")

councils cap in full title, eg, Birmingham City Council, otherwise l/c

council tax replacement for poll tax/community charge, so use the latter only in their historical context

counsel is both singular and plural in court contexts. Do not say "counsels for Mr X and Mrs Y". *See* Courts special section (page 47)

counter-productive, counter-attack etc, but **countertenor** (one word)

counties spell out names except in lists. Do not add -shire to Devon (except in Devonshire cream or the Duke of Devonshire), Dorset,

Somerset. Irish counties should be as Co Donegal (cap "C", no full point); Co Durham takes the same style. Take great care with new, reorganised or abolished counties. *See* Durham, unitary authorities

Courchevel, the Alpine ski resort (not Courcheval)

court martial plural, courts martial, Courts-Martial Appeal Court; verb, to court-martial

Court of Appeal always use the full title at first mention and wherever possible thereafter, though appeal court (l/c) may be used sparingly. *See* Courts special section (page 47)

Court of Arches is the court of appeal of the Province of Canterbury in the Church of England. Do not say Arches Court

Court of St James's

Court of Session, Edinburgh (not Sessions)

Court Service, the (caps; not Courts)

courts cap all courts when specific, eg, Birmingham Crown Court, Clerkenwell County Court, Dawlish Magistrates' Court, Ashford Youth Court etc; in a general, unspecific context, always cap the Crown Court (it sits in about 90 centres), but l/c county court, magistrates' court or youth court etc. *See* Courts special section (page 47); also

coroner's court; Crown Court; Inns of Court

Coutts Bank

Coward, Noël (use the diaeresis)

crackdown not banned, but use as little as possible

Cracow (not Krakow or variations). *See* foreign places

crèche (not créche)

creditworthy, creditworthiness (no hyphen)

Creole is a person born in the West Indies or Latin America whose ancestry is wholly or partly European. It does not imply mixed race

crescendo means getting louder, growing in force. Nothing *rises* to a *crescendo*. Plural is crescendos

Cresta Run

Creutzfeldt-Jakob disease (abbreviate CJD). Note also variant CJD (with l/c "v"), abbreviated to vCJD. No longer call it new variant CJD

crisis always try to find an alternative for this greatly overworked word. Its use should be confined to a process reaching a turning point. A crisis does not deepen, grow, mount or worsen, and is never a continuous state such as a "housing crisis". Economics are never "in crisis"; "crisis situations" are *never* to appear in *The Times*

THE COURTS

1. **Criminal cases**: Most of these are dealt with by magistrates' courts, presided over by magistrates, who are lay justices (JPs). The busiest have full-time paid judges, formerly called stipendiaries but now known as district judges (magistrates' courts). Refer to them simply as District Judge Joe Smith etc. The more serious criminal cases are heard in the Crown Court, of which the most famous (in the City of London) is the Central Criminal Court, or Old Bailey (either form acceptable). Always cap Crown Court and never use crown courts in the plural

2. **Civil cases**: These are heard in magistrates' courts and county courts, the more serious in the High Court, which has three divisions – the Queen's Bench, Chancery, and Family Divisions (cap Division in full title). In London they are based at the Royal Courts of Justice in the Strand.

    The Divisional Court of the Queen's Bench Division can quash decisions by magistrates' courts and hear appeals from lower courts on points of law. It is also the court for reviewing governmental bodies' or local authorities' decisions – judicial review. Distinguish between applications for leave and the main hearing

3. **Court of Appeal**: always use the full title at first mention and wherever possible thereafter, though appeal court (l/c) may be used sparingly. The court sits with three judges, who are Lords Justices of Appeal. The highest court in the land is the **Judicial Committee of the House of Lords** (though normally the House of Lords or simply the law lords [l/c] will suffice); they are the most senior judges, formally called the Lords of Appeal in Ordinary

4. **Scottish courts**: Court of Session, Edinburgh (for civil actions); High Court of Justiciary (prosecution of serious crimes and criminal appeals); the senior judge is Lord President (of the Court of Session) and also Lord Justice-General (in High Court); others are Lord Justice-Clerk (in both) and, formally, Lords of Session and Lords Commissioners of Justiciary. Sheriff (not sheriff's) Courts deal with less serious criminal and civil cases.

    Other points in Scotland: advocate (equivalent of English barrister); the Crown prosecutors are the Lord Advocate and Advocates-Depute and (in each sheriffdom) the Procurator Fiscal (plural, Procurators

Fiscal); in civil actions, pursuer (equivalent of plaintiff), defender (the defendant), summons (writ containing pursuer's case)

5. Note that **youth courts** have replaced the old juvenile courts

JUDGES

In magistrates' courts, the **bench** is always l/c

The **district judge** replaced the old county court registrar and is referred to (at first mention) as District Judge Fred Brown

At the Central Criminal Court, the **Recorder** of the City of London is usually referred to as "the Recorder". Note caps for the **Common Serjeant**. The Recorder of London, Recorder of Liverpool and Recorder of Manchester (and no other places) are circuit judges and are referred to at first mention as Judge Michael Bean, Recorder of Manchester etc (thereafter the recorder, not Mr Recorder)

A **circuit judge** sits either in the Crown Court or in the county court and should be referred to as Judge Joe Bean, QC, (the QC where appropriate). Circuit judges may also sit in the High Court, in which case they should be described as "Judge Joe Bean, sitting as a High Court judge . . ."

High Court judges should be referred to as Mr (or Mrs) Justice Bean throughout. Christian (or first) names are not normally necessary unless there are two or more High Court judges with the same surname, where it is essential to differentiate. These judges have a knighthood and may also be described as Sir John Bean, Dame Eleanor Bean etc, but generally only out of the court context

Court of Appeal judges are Lords Justices of Appeal. Use Lord Justice Bean throughout, or out of court context, Sir John Bean. Note **Lady Justice Butler-Sloss**, although now she is President of the Family Division, she is styled **Dame Elizabeth Butler-Sloss**. Also Lord Justice **Brooke** (not Brook)

House of Lords, or **law lords**, the most senior judges, are the Lords of Appeal in Ordinary. Call them Lord Bean, in or out of court; first mention, give full title, eg, Lord Bean of Muckleflugga, thereafter Lord Bean. When writing about their judgments, say "the House of Lords ruled" or "the law lords ruled".

Retired judges should be referred to as follows:

a. Retired High Court judges, Sir Ivan Parsons

b. retired Crown Court judges, George Vickers, QC, (first mention), then Mr Vickers

COURT REPORTING

1. **In general**, use l/c for titles etc except when in full or specific; thus, Anthony Bloggs, QC, the Recorder (thereafter the recorder), the West London Magistrate, Chelmsford Crown Court, Horseferry Road Magistrates' Court, Dawlish Magistrates' Court (caps on first mention), etc; but "the court was told", "the judge said", "the magistrate ordered" etc. **The Bench is capped only when referring to the judges as a group; a bench of magistrates is always l/c. Always cap the Bar and the Inn** (even when used on its own)

2. **Criminal cases**: lawyers here appear "for the prosecution", "for the defence" (avoid "prosecuting", "defending"). To "admit" or "deny" an offence is preferred to "pleads guilty" or "pleads not guilty", though the latter form is not banned.

   Seek legal guidance before naming anybody under 17 in any court case.

   Do not report details of sex offences involving children and do not allow sex trial reports to become surreptitious pornography.

   Also, do not identify any victims of alleged sexual offences.

   At the end of a court report, say if the trial – or the hearing, in a civil case – continues. *Always* give the verdict at the end of a trial or hearing.

   Defendants take their Mr, Mrs etc until they are convicted (*see* appellations, paragraph f)

3. **Civil cases**: the parties in civil cases are the claimant (formerly the plaintiff) and the defendant. Say "counsel for Mrs Y" rather than "counsel for the claimant" etc. In judicial review, the person challenging the decision is the applicant

4. **Appeals**: in criminal cases, the defendant becomes the appellant; the respondent is usually the Crown. Say "counsel for Mr Smith" rather than "counsel for the appellant". In civil appeals, either the claimant (formerly plaintiff) or the defendant can be the appellant; it is always better to identify the parties and then avoid the phrase *counsel for the appellant/respondent* wherever possible

5. **Legal officers**: cap Official Solicitor, Treasury Solicitor, Senior Official Receiver (but note l/c official receiver, because there are several). These should be distinguished from the **law officers**, who are the Attorney-General and the Solicitor-General

6. The **Director of Public Prosecutions** (DPP) heads the Crown Prosecution Service (CPS), whose lawyers are Crown prosecutors

7. **Solicitors**: never refer to a "company" of solicitors – they are always "firms". Always omit Messrs before the firm's name, eg, simply Sue, Grabbit & Runne

8. **Law Report** cases cited go in italics, eg, *Gornall v Ritter* and in *Gornall's* case. In news reports and features, roman should be retained

9. **Inns of Court** order of precedence is Lincoln's Inn, Inner Temple, Middle Temple, Gray's Inn

10. **Coroner's court**: at inquests, the coroner is l/c unless specific, as in the Westminster Coroner. Juries **return the verdict, the coroner records it**. Be careful not to describe pathologists automatically as a Home Office pathologist – most are private consultants, so always check and use simply "the pathologist" if in doubt. There are no coroner's inquests in Scotland: sudden deaths are reported to the Procurator Fiscal, who may hold a fatal accident inquiry

11. **Latin phrases** go in roman, eg, mandamus, habeas corpus, certiorari etc, but maxims take italic, eg, *caveat emptor*

12. An important reminder: in court reports, it is *Times* style to use the phrases **for the prosecution** and **for the defence**, rather than simply prosecuting and defending

13. **silk**: barristers take silk and become silks (all l/c)

14. **recorders**: when part-time judges, barristers or solicitors are sitting as recorders, refer to them as, eg, Donald Williams, QC, (where

appropriate) the Recorder (later mentions, Mr Williams or the recorder); never say Mr Recorder Williams etc

15. **small claims court** (l/c, as not its official title)

16. **Criminal Bar** (caps); similarly, the **Commercial Bar** etc

17. **"no win, no fee"** legislation/agreement etc

18. **commercial court** l/c, as not an official division of the High Court (unlike the Family Division, Queen's Bench Division etc)

19. guidelines on **when to cap courts**: cap all courts when specific, eg Birmingham Crown Court, Clerkenwell County Court, Dawlish Magistrates' Court, Ashford Youth Court etc; in a general, unspecific context, always cap the High Court, and the Crown Court (it sits in about 90 centres); but l/c county court, magistrates' court, youth court etc

20. cap **President of the Law Society** and **Chairman of the Bar Council**

21. **Office for the Supervision of Solicitors** (no longer the Solicitors Complaints Bureau)

22. new legal bodies or services (from 1999): **Legal Services Commission**; **Community Legal Service**; **Criminal Defence Service** (all caps)

23. **Woolf reforms** In April 1999 new procedural rules for the conduct of civil litigation came into force, including important changes of terminology. These include:
    - a plaintiff is now a **claimant**
    - a writ is now a **claim form**
    - all pleadings are **statements of case**
    - affidavits become very rare; most written evidence will simply be verified by a **statement of truth**
    - **notices of application** will be served in the place of summonses. The means by which justice will be speeded up and administered is **allocation** to the appropriate track: the **small claims track** (up to £5,000), the **fast track** (up to £15,000), and the **multitrack** (the rest)

24. **"magic circle"**, l/c and quotes at first mention, for top City law firms

INTERNATIONAL COURTS

a. **The International Court of Justice** sits in The Hague. It is the judicial organ of the UN and only states can be parties there.

b. **The European Court of Justice** is the shortened (and usual) form of the Court of Justice of the European Communities, and sits in Luxembourg. The Advocate General (caps, no hyphen) sits in the European Court; he presents the case to the court and delivers an opinion, then the court makes its judgment.

c. **The Court of Auditors** (which sits in Luxembourg) is the fifth institution of the EU, under the Maastricht treaty. (The others are the Council of the European Union, the European Commission, the European Court of Justice and the European Parliament.)

d. **The European Court of Human Rights** sits in Strasbourg. It is the judicial body of the Council of Europe **(not an EC or EU body)**; the human rights court rules on cases brought against states under the Convention for the Protection of Human Rights and Fundamental Freedoms, usually referred to as the **European Convention on Human Rights**. From November 1998, the European Court of Human Rights has incorporated the former European Commission of Human Rights, which no longer exists.

In the Strasbourg context note that neither the Parliamentary Assembly of the Council of Europe nor the Committee of Ministers of the Council of Europe is an EU institution.

---

criterion plural criteria

Croat for the people and language, **Croatian** for the general adjective. *See* Slovak, Slovakian

Cross, the (cap). *See* Christian terms

cross benches, but crossbenchers, crossbench opinion

cross-Channel, but transatlantic

Crown (in constitutional sense) is capped, as in Crown property, the Crown representative. *See* Royal Family

Crown Court always cap and do not refer to crown courts (plural) as there is technically only the Crown Court, which may sit in any of some 90 centres. *See* Courts special section (page 47)

Crown Estate Commissioners (not Estates)

Crown Jewels (caps)

Crown Prosecution Service (CPS)

Crufts Show, or just Crufts (no apostrophe)

cruise missiles, but Pershing missiles and the Stealth bomber

crunch avoid phrases such as *reaches crunch point, the situation came to a crunch* – clichés that have no place in *The Times*

CSCE no longer. *See* OSCE

Cup cap *Final* only in FA Cup Final (or Cup Final for short), but l/c all others, such as European Cup final, World Cup final, Davis Cup final etc. *See* Sports special section (page 160)

cupfuls, spoonfuls etc (not cupsful or cupfulls)

currencies always convert to sterling on news, sport and features pages – usually at first mention of the foreign currency. But on Business pages, commonly used foreign currencies need not be converted, unless to help the flow of the story. *See* deutschemark, dollars, euro, franc and peseta

current avoid wherever possible as synonym of *present*

curriculums (plural, not curricula; but note extracurricular activities); **curriculum vitae, CV** abbreviated (plural, **curricula vitae**). *See* national curriculum

curtsy (not curtsey); plural **curtsies**

Custom House (the headquarters building)

Customs and Excise cap for the organisation (or simply Customs), l/c for customs officer, customs post, customs regulations etc

cut-throat use hyphen

Cyprus, northern keep the l/c in northern, as the "state" is recognised only by the Turkish Government; also l/c government in northern Cyprus, as with provincial or state governments in Australia or Canada etc

czar although usual style is tsar (in Russian context), the czar form is permissible in the context of government-appointed co-ordinators such as drugs czar, mental health czar. *See* tsar

Czech Republic use Czechoslovakia only in the historic sense. The two countries since their division are the Czech Republic and Slovakia

D

dad and **mum** caps when referring to specific parents, l/c in general context

Dagestan (not Daghestan)

Dail Eireann the lower house of the Irish parliament; usually just the Dail

Dales, the Yorkshire (cap); or just the Dales

dance. *See* Arts special section (page 18)

dancefloor

Dar es Salaam, Tanzania (no hyphens). Note, capital is Dodoma

Dark Ages caps, but take care; the period after the fall of the Roman Empire is no longer considered wholly obscure and barbaric

Darwin, Charles write the title of his great work as *On the Origin of Species* (usually omitting the words *by Means of Natural Selection*)

data strictly plural, but can now be used in singular through common usage

databank, **database**

date rape beware of this phrase; in most cases "drug rape" is the intended meaning

dates Monday, April 18, 1994 (never 18th April); but April 1994. When citing periods of years, say 1992–93 (not 1992–3); for the new millennium, write 1999–2000, then 2000–01, 2003–09 etc; from 1939 to 1941 (not from 1939–41); the **Forties**, **Eighties**, **Nineties** (or 1940s, 1980s, 1990s). But with people's ages, l/c, as in "she was in her forties, eighties, nineties" etc. Common usage says that the last century ended on December 31, 1999. *See* millennium

Day-Glo (caps, proprietary)

daytime, but **night-time**

day trader, **day trading** (no need to hyphenate)

day trip, but **day-tripper**

D-Day, **VE-Day**, **VJ-Day**

deathbed (no hyphen)

death row (as in American prisons), l/c

debacle (accents unnecessary)

debatable

Debrett, or full title *Debrett's Peerage*

debut (no accent)

decades use either the Sixties or the 1960s. *See* dates

de Chastelain, General John
(l/c de)

decimals do not mix decimals and fractions in the same story. *See* metric, millions, per cent

decimate means to kill one in ten; custom has extended its use to indicate heavy casualties, but use sparingly

deckchair, as armchair (no hyphens)

decor (no accent)

decorations. *See* honours

defuse means to remove the fuse from, or reduce tension in an emergency etc; never confuse with **diffuse**, which means to spread in all directions, scatter etc, or (as adjective) verbose, not concise, spread over a large area etc

Degas (no accent)

de Gaulle never cap *de* in this name unless at the start of a sentence or headline

de Havilland

de Klerk, F. W. *See* full points

de la Mare, Walter

De La Rue

DeLorean

De Niro, Robert

de Sancha, Antonia (former friend of David Mellor)

de Valera, Eamon

degrees (educational) a first, a second, an upper second (a 2:1), a lower second (a 2:2), a third etc. Abbreviations as follows: doctorates of literature (or letters), D Lit, D Litt, LitD etc; Oxford and York have D Phil instead of the more usual PhD. Oxford has DM for the more usual MD. Cambridge has ScD for doctor of science. No full points in degrees

degrees (weather) omit degree sign in temperatures. *See* celsius

déjà vu (accents but not italic)

deliver this word has become a cliché, particularly in political stories, so always try to think of an alternative; eg, promises are kept, policies are implemented, public services are provided, improvements are made

Deloitte & Touche can be shortened to Deloitte after first mention

demise strictly means the death of a person, or the failure of an enterprise or institution. Keep to these definitions. It is wrong to refer to the demise of Glenn Hoddle or Peter Mandelson

Democratic Party (US), not Democrat Party. The adjective is usually Democrat in other uses, such as the Democrat spokesman (but note the Democratic convention)

demonstration never shorten to *demo* except in direct quotes

demonstrator, but *see* protester

Deng, Wendi Rupert Murdoch's wife. *See* Murdoch

Denktas, Rauf (not Denktash), the president (l/c) of northern Cyprus (l/c because not an internationally recognised state); better to describe him as *the Turkish Cypriot leader*. *See* Cyprus

deny does not mean the same as **rebut** (which means argue to the contrary, producing evidence), or **refute** (which means to win such an argument). *See* rebut, refute

departments (government) all the reorganised government departments since the June 2001 general election incorporate "for" in their names (not "of"):
- **Department for Education and Skills** (DfES after first mention);
- **Department for Environment, Food and Rural Affairs** (not **the** Environment), Defra after first mention;
- **Department for Transport** (no longer, since May 2002, the Department for Transport, Local Government and the Regions). The responsibility for local government and the regions now comes under the Office of the Deputy Prime Minister;
- **Department for Work and Pensions**.

Longer-established departments with the same style are the

Department for Culture, Media and Sport; and the **Department for International Development**

dependant (noun), **dependent** (adj), **dependency**

Depression, the cap for the 1930s economic slump

Deputy Prime Minister (caps); similarly, Deputy Governor of the Bank of England. But these are the exceptions to the rule that deputy posts should normally take the l/c, eg, deputy editor

desiccate

desktop (computer, publishing), no hyphen. *See* laptop

despite perfectly acceptable alternative for *in spite of*. But do not say "despite the fact that"; use *although* instead

despoiled (not despoilt)

despoliation or **despoilment** (not despoilation)

deutschemark/deutschmark prefer not to use either form, nor D-mark. Use simply the mark, or with figures, DM500 (all now in historic contexts). *See* currencies

Deutsche Bank German commercial bank not to be confused with Deutsche Bundesbank, or Bundesbank, the German central bank

Devil, the (cap); but **devils** (many, l/c), **devilish**

dextrous (prefer to dexterous)

Dhaka (not Dacca), capital of Bangladesh

Diaghilev

diagnose take great care: illnesses are diagnosed, patients are not

Diana, Princess of Wales, at first mention; subsequently the Princess (cap, as she remained a member of the Royal Family until her death). Still never say Princess Diana or – even worse – Princess Di (except in reported speech). Now say the late Princess where appropriate. Note **the Diana, Princess of Wales Memorial Fund** (one comma only). *See* Royal Family, Titles special section (page 171)

Diaspora cap in Jewish context, but l/c in general sense of a dispersal

Di Canio, Paolo (cap Di every time)

DiCaprio, Leonardo

Dickins & Jones (department store)

Dictaphone is a trade name and must be capped

diehard (no hyphen)

dietitian (prefer to dietician)

different from, and *never* different *to* or *than*; likewise, differ from

dignitaries

dilapidated (not delapidated)

dilate dilation means normal widening, as in pupils of the eye; dilatation is widening by force, as in child abuse cases. Take care

dining room (no hyphen)

Dinky Toys cap T (trademark), but Dinky on its own can be sufficient

diocese cap in specifics, such as Diocese of Chichester or the Guildford Diocese, but l/c in general use, and l/c **diocesan**. *See* Churches special section (page 37)

diphtheria, **diphthong** (note "ph")

Diplomatic Service (caps, as Civil Service)

directives (in EU) l/c in general context, caps when specific, eg, Working Time Directive

Direct Line and Direct Line Insurance are trademarks and must not be used in a generic sense even with l/c, as in *direct line companies*, *direct line telephone insurers* etc; in this wider sense, say *direct insurance*, *direct telephone insurance* etc

Director of Public Prosecutions (DPP)

Director-General of the BBC, CBI, Institute of Directors, Fair Trading, and the regulatory bodies etc. *See* regulators, Secretary-General

Directory Enquiries (despite usual style, inquiries)

disc (musical, recording, or shape, eg, disc jockey, compact disc, disc brake); but **disk** in general computing context, eg, disk drive, floppy disk

discomfit take great care with this verb; it means primarily to thwart, defeat or rout, but by extension can mean thoroughly to embarrass or disconcert (noun discomfiture). It has no connection with discomfort, which means to deprive of comfort or make uneasy

discreet means tactful, circumspect (noun discretion); **discrete** means individually distinct (noun discreteness)

disinterested means impartial, unbiased (noun disinterest); never confuse with **uninterested**, which means having a lack of interest

disk. *See* disc

Disney the theme parks are **Disneyland** (California); **Disney World** (Florida); **Disneyland Paris** (Euro Disney should strictly be confined to the name of the European company); and **Tokyo Disneyland** (owned by a Japanese company, but Disney earns royalties from it)

disorientate (not disorient). *See* orientate

dispatch (not despatch), including **dispatch box**

dissociate (not disassociate)

distil, distilled, distillation

divorcé, man; **divorcée**, woman; use **divorcees** (no accent) in reference to both men and women

DIY spell out do-it-yourself at first mention

D-notice, D-notice committee

Docklands in London, docklands elsewhere

doctor the title Dr should no longer be confined to medical practitioners. If a person has a doctorate from a reputable institution, and wishes to be known as Dr Smith, he or she should be so titled. *See* appellations

docusoap, **docudrama** etc (no hyphens)

dogfight, as bullfight, cockfight etc

dogs l/c with most breeds, such as alsatian, borzoi, labrador, rottweiler, though there are obvious exceptions such as West Highland terrier, Yorkshire terrier, Jack Russell etc

Dole, Bob (not Robert)

dollars with figures use $5 (when American), A$5 (Australian), C$5 (Canadian), S$5 (Singapore)

doll's house (not dolls')

Dolly the sheep (l/c "s")

Dome cap "D" in Millennium Dome and when used on its own, whether as noun or adjective. *See* millennium

Domesday Book (roman, like Magna Carta), but **doomsday** in general or biblical sense

Dominican Republic, neighbour to Haiti, while **Dominica** is one of the Windward Islands. Both are sovereign states. *See* Haiti

donate use *give* or *present* wherever possible

Dorchester, the (not Dorchester Hotel)

do's and don'ts

Dostoevsky

dot-com use hyphen for colloquial reference to internet companies

doveish (rather than dovish)

down avoid unnecessary use after verbs, as in close down, shut down. *See* up

Downing Street write 10 Downing Street (or 11 …), or simply No 10; note Downing Street policy unit. *See* Politics special section (page 131); *also see* units

Downing Street declaration. *See* Ireland

downmarket (no hyphen), as upmarket

Down's syndrome never say mongol

Down Under cap as a colloquialism for Australasia (especially Australia)

D'Oyly Carte

drachmas, not drachmae (now historical contexts)

draconian (l/c)

draftsman (legal), but **draughtsman** (art, design)

drama, **dramatic** confine their use to the theatrical context wherever possible; *dramatic events* and the like are among the tiredest clichés in the language

Dr Dolittle (italics for the film, roman for the character)

dreamt, not dreamed

drier is the comparative of dry; **dryer** is the noun, as in tumble dryer

drink-drive, drink–driver, drink–driving. Note that the limits are 35 **micrograms** of alcohol per 100 millilitres of **breath**; and 80 **milligrams** of alcohol per 100 millilitres of **blood**

drivers no hyphens in taxi driver, bus driver, car driver etc

drop a bombshell never in *The Times*

dropout (noun or adjective – as in students); **drop-out** (rugby); and to **drop out** (verb)

drugs do not confuse narcotics (which include cocaine and heroin) with other illicit drugs such as cannabis, LSD and amphetamines

Drug Enforcement Administration (US), thereafter DEA

Druid(s) (cap)

Druze (in Lebanon)

Dr Who, roman for the character (subsequent mentions, the Doctor), but italics for the programme

dry-clean, **dry-cleaning** etc

drystone wall

dual (of two, eg, dual carriageway); **duel** (fight)

du Cann, Sir Edward

Duchess of York she is no longer a member of the Royal Family since her divorce. After her first mention as Duchess of York, refer to the duchess (l/c) subsequently – never "Fergie" or any such vulgarity. See Titles special section (page 131)

due to must *not* be used as the equivalent of *because of* or *owing to*. The phrase must be attached to a noun or pronoun: "His absence was due to illness" is correct; "He was absent due to illness" is wrong

duffel bag, **duffel coat**

Duke of Edinburgh say the Duke (cap) or Prince Philip after first mention; but this cap rule applies only to the British Royal Family and overseas heads of state, so the Duke of Rutland would become the duke (l/c) after first mention. See Royal Family, heads of state, titles

dump do not use as synonym of dismiss or sack

Durham say Co Durham for the county and (if any question of ambiguity) Durham city for the city. See counties

duty-free (hyphenated, noun or adjective)

DVLA, the Driver and Vehicle Licensing Agency (not Authority)

dwarf as plural, prefer dwarfs (not dwarves); avoid "politically correct" circumlocutions such as "person of restricted growth"

dyke (embankment), not dike

dysentery (not dysentry or disentery)

dyspepsia

E

each, **every** although singular, they are acceptable now with plural pronouns, as the plural is increasingly becoming a way of saying *he* or *she*, or *his* or *her*. Hence, "everyone has what they want", "each of us has our secrets", but "everyone has secrets"

Earhart, Amelia (the 1930s aviatrix)

Earls Court (no apostrophe)

early hours avoid the phrase "in the early hours of the morning"; say simply "the early hours" or, better, "early yesterday/today"

earned never *earnt*

earring (no hyphen)

Earth cap only in planetary or astronomical sense, not in phrases such as "down to earth". The same rule applies to Moon and Sun. *See* Universe

earthquake can abbreviate to *quake* in headings. *See* Richter scale

east, **eastern** etc for when to cap in geographical context, *see* compass points

East End, West End of London; also East, West, North, South, Central, Inner London. *See* London

EastEnders (the TV soap opera)

Easter Day (not Easter Sunday)

Eastern Europe, but eastern Germany. *See* Germany

easygoing

easyJet note also buzz and Go

ebitda earnings before interest, tax, depreciation and amortisation; where possible spell out at first mention

EBRD European Bank for Reconstruction and Development

EC must *not* be used as an abbreviation for the European Commission in text or headlines. EC remains the short form *only* of the European Community, although in almost all contexts now, EU is preferred. *See* European etc

E. coli (italics in text, but roman and no point in headlines)

e-commerce (as e-mail)

ecosystem (no hyphen), but **eco-warrior**

Ecstasy, the drug

Ecuadorean (not –ian)

ecumenical, not oecumenical (but respect titles). *See* Churches special section (page 37)

editor cap first mention of editors

of well-known leading publications, such as the Editor of *The Times*, Editor of the *Daily Mirror*, Editor of the *Yorkshire Post*, Editor of *The Spectator*; subsequent mentions, revert to l/c. Similarly, Editor-in-Chief. Note that deputy editors and below retain l/c. *See* job titles, newspapers

education action zones (EAZs), l/c in general context but cap specifics, eg, Barnsley Education Action Zone. Similar style to **local education authorities (LEAs)**

educationist (not educationalist)

, eg, no points, but use a comma before and after. *See* ie

Eid ul-Fitr, the festival marking the end of the fast of Ramadan

Eire do not use except in historical context. *See* Ireland

eisteddfod l/c except when naming a particular one in full, eg, the International Eisteddfod at Llangollen; plural eisteddfodau

either takes a singular verb when both subjects are embraced: "Either is good enough." *See* neither

elbowroom (one word), similarly headroom, legroom

elderly, **aged**, **old** be sensitive in the use of these words, and generally do not use for people under 65

Electoral College cap in US election context

electrocardiographs are machines for measuring heart function; electrocardiograms are the tracings made by them

electrocute means to kill by electric shock

Elgin Marbles, and subsequent mentions the Marbles

elicit means to evoke, bring to light, or draw out; never confuse with **illicit** (unlawful, forbidden)

Eliot, T(homas) S(tearns), usually known as T. S. Eliot; also **George Eliot** (real name Mary Ann Evans)

elite (roman, no accent)

e-mail, but note E-Stamp, a registered trademark

embarkation (not embarcation). You embark *in* (not on) a ship. *See* Armed Forces special section (page 14)

embarrass(ment); but note the French *embarras de choix*, *embarras de richesses*

Embassy same style as for Ambassador, eg, the French Embassy in Rome, thereafter the embassy

émigré

Emin, Tracey (not Tracy)

Emmies (plural of the Emmy awards). *See* arts awards

emphasise prefer this to *stress* in phrases such as "he emphasised the importance", "she emphasised that the ruling was final". *See* stress

empire cap as in British or Roman Empire; similarly, cap **emperor** when specific, eg, Emperor Claudius

Employment Appeal Tribunal (note singular Appeal) is part of the High Court and should be referred to in full at first mention, then the appeal tribunal (not simply the tribunal). It is not the same as an employment tribunal, which replaced the old industrial tribunal and which can be referred to as the tribunal at second mention. *See* next entry

employment tribunals have replaced industrial tribunals. *See* industrial

EMS European Monetary System

EMU economic and monetary union (in Europe). *See* ERM

encyclopaedia (not encyclopedia)

England, English beware of these when the meaning is Britain, British

England and Wales Cricket Board, which has replaced the TCCB, is abbreviated as **ECB**, but do not shorten to England/English Cricket Board. *See* Sports special section (page 160)

engineers restrict use to white-collar workers with engineering qualifications; do not use with reference to mechanics, manufacturing workers, platelayers etc

enormity does *not* mean great size; it means quality or character of being outrageous, or extreme wickedness or serious error. Do not misuse. For great size, use **immensity**

en route (not italics)

ensign the **White Ensign** is the ensign of the Royal Navy and the Royal Yacht Squadron; the **Red Ensign** is the British Merchant Navy's flag; the **Blue Ensign** is flown by Royal Fleet Auxiliary vessels and by certain yacht clubs. There is no such thing as the Royal Ensign; however, the **Royal Standard** will fly from one of the Queen's homes when she is there. *See* Royal Standard

en suite (two words, no hyphen, no itals, both as adverb and adjective)

ensure means to make certain; you **insure** against risk; you **assure** your life. The verb **ensure** usually needs "that" after it if accompanied by a following verb (eg, "he tried to ensure that the policy was adopted"); but omit "that" if followed by a noun (eg, "he tried to ensure its success")

enthral

Environment Agency (caps)

eponymous means "giving its

name to …" so "Hamlet, the eponymous Prince" (ie, giving his name to the play) is correct; "*Hamlet*, the eponymous play", is wrong

Equator (cap), but **equatorial** in general sense

Eriksson, Sven-Göran (England football head coach, not manager); note hyphen and umlaut

ERM exchange-rate mechanism (in European contexts); a part of the wider concept of EMU

escalate, **escalation** now clichés, so avoid; use *rise*, *grow* or *soar*

escapers never *escapees*

Eskimo is now regarded as a derogatory term. Use **Inuit** instead, except in occasional historical contexts

Establishment, the cap in sense of the perceived leaders of society; but l/c as in the medical establishment, the legal establishment, when the sense is more restricted

Eta (not ETA), the Basque separatist organisation. Note also Basque Country (initial caps)

Eucharist (cap). *See* Christian terms

euro, the European single currency, takes l/c (as franc, pound, mark, peseta etc)

eurocheques, **eurobonds** (l/c, no hyphen)

euroland (l/c), vernacular term for European single currency area; also **eurozone**

Europe Western, Eastern, Central (all caps). Europe includes the British Isles, so do not use the name as equivalent to the Continent. Britain does not export to Europe, but to the *rest* of Europe

European Commission, **Commissioners** cap the Commission throughout as a noun, but l/c when adjectival, eg, *a commission ruling* (the same rule as for Government/government); cap the commissioner only when referring to a specific person (eg, Mario Monti, the Competition Commissioner; thereafter, the commissioner). The President of the European Commission is capped throughout (as with all foreign Presidents)

European Economic Area (EEA), the European tariff-free zone, comprises the 15 members of the EU plus Norway, Iceland and Liechtenstein. Other EU-EEA areas of co-operation include education, research, environment, consumer policy and tourism

European Parliament, Members of the European Parliament (MEPs), or Euro MPs

European Union (EU), **European Community (EC)** the first is now the preferred phrase except where the context is trade. If we have to use *the Union*, it should be capped throughout, but wherever possible use EU. Use Common Market and EEC only in historical context

Eurosceptic (no longer hyphenated), and similarly **Europhobia, Europhiles**. Write Eurosceptic with capital E for anti-European in general sense, **eurosceptic** (l/c "e") for those who oppose the euro (single currency)

Eurotunnel (one word) is the company that owns and operates the Channel Tunnel. **Eurostar** operates the passenger trains that run through the tunnel. Note that **Eurotunnel trains** carry cars, coaches and lorries through the tunnel between Calais and Folkestone only; they run a shuttle service and although the logo of Le Shuttle still appears on their locomotives, their formal name is Eurotunnel trains. *See* Channel Tunnel

evangelical(s) keep l/c in general church contexts except when part of an official title such as the Evangelical Alliance

evensong (l/c). *See* matins, Christian terms

eventuate avoid; use *happen* instead

ever is rarely necessary; avoid phrases such as *best-ever, fastest-ever*, and say simply *best* and *fastest*, qualifying (where appropriate) with

yet. *See* first, superlatives, universal claims

ex- prefer *former* in most contexts, as in *former Yugoslavia*, though ex-serviceman is unavoidable and ex- is fine for headlines

examinations 11-plus, 7-plus etc; also A levels, but A-level results etc (hyphenate only when adjectival); also AS levels, A2s. Abbreviate to *exam* only in headlines. GCSE, the General Certificate of Secondary Education, need not normally be spelt out. *See* A level, GCSE

excepting do not use when *except* or *except for* is possible

exclamation marks nearly always unnecessary

exclusive avoid with story or interview. The phrase "in an interview with *The Times*" is sufficient

ex dividend (not ex-dividend) in financial contexts

execution take care; as with assassination, do not use as a synonym of any killing or murder. An execution is a judicial killing after due process of law

Executive cap in the Scottish, Welsh and Northern Ireland contexts when used as a noun meaning the Government; but l/c when adjectival (same style as for Government, Assembly, Commission etc)

exhibitions titles of art exhibitions in italics. *See* Arts special section (page 18)

exlsting use *present* wherever possible as an alternative

Exocet (cap)

expatriate (noun, verb or adjective – not *ex-patriate* and never *expatriot*)

Export Credits Guarantee Department (ECGD) (note Credits plural)

extramarital (no hyphen); similarly, **extramural**,

extracurricular, **extrasensory** etc

exuberant (never exhuberant), but **exhilarate**, **exhort** etc

eye of a storm do not refer to "the calm in the eye of the storm"; the eye, by definition, is the calm area at the centre of a storm or hurricane

eye to eye (no hyphens)

eyeing

eyewitness use witness instead wherever possible (except in direct quotes)

F

F111s (no hyphen). *See* aircraft types

façade (use the cedilla)

facelift use sparingly in its metaphorical sense, where it has become overworked. In its cosmetic context quite acceptable, however

fact sheet

fact that almost always an unnecessary circumlocution, so avoid (eg, "owing to the fact that" means *because*)

Faeroe Isles, or the Faeroes

fahrenheit. *See* celsius

fairytale no hyphen

Faithfull, Marianne

falangist in Spain; **phalangist** in Lebanon

fallacy means a faulty argument, not an erroneous belief

Fallopian tubes (cap "F")

fallout (noun)

Far East encompasses the following: China, Hong Kong, Japan, North and South Korea, Macau, Mongolia, Taiwan. *See* Asean, South-East Asia

farther is applied only to distance (literal or figurative); eg, "nothing could be farther from the truth".
Further means *in addition to*, *another*, eg, "a further point"

fascia (not facia)

Fascist cap in the political sense, but as a term of abuse, l/c; but **fascism** l/c except in specifically party context. *See* communism

Father (as in priest) avoid the ugly abbreviation Fr before a name

Father's Day (not Fathers'). *See* Mother's Day

fatwa (not italic), a Muslim religious edict, not a sentence of punishment

fault-line (hyphen)

Fayed, Dodi (not Dodi Al Fayed), the late elder son of Mohamed Al Fayed

Fed, the (US) say Federal Reserve (Board not usually necessary) at first mention; cap the Chairman of the Fed, as with Governor of the Bank of England, President of the Bundesbank etc

Federal Aviation Administration (FAA) (in US); not *Agency* or *Authority*

Federation of Small Businesses (not Business)

feel-good factor (no longer use quotes)

Fellow cap in specific title such as Dr Arthur Brown, a Fellow of Magdalen, or in the more obvious Fellow of the Royal College of Surgeons (FRCS); but in general sense, "a group of fellows in the quadrangle", l/c; keep fellowship l/c

female do not write female councillors, female directors etc; say women councillors, women directors

feminine designations, such as authoress, poetess, wardress, should be avoided. But actress is such common usage that it is acceptable. *See* comedienne

Ferris wheel

Festival Hall generally omit Royal

festivals cap the Edinburgh Festival (cultural), Reading Festival (pop), Cheltenham Festival (racing) etc, thereafter the festival (l/c). *See* Fringe

fête (with accent)

fewer, of numbers (fewer people, fewer goals); **less**, of size, in quantity, or singular nouns (less population, less meat). *See* less

fiancé (man), **fiancée** (woman). *See* divorcé

Fianna Fail; **Fine Gael**. *See* Ireland

Fide (not FIDE), the world chess body. *See* chess names

fifty write 50–50 chance; note Fifties (cap) for the decade, but "she was in her fifties" (age, l/c)

fighting for his/her life avoid this meaningless phrase. Instead say *critically ill/injured*

figures. *See* numbers

filibuster (not fillibuster)

Filipinos, **Filipinas** (women), **the Philippines**

films titles in italics (*see* Arts special section, page 18); note **film-maker**. *See* movies

film star (two words)

Filofax (proprietary, *must* cap). Use "personal organiser" for generic

Financial Ombudsman Service (not Service Ombudsman). *See* ombudsman

Financial Services Authority (FSA) has replaced the Securities and Investments Board. *See* Personal Investment Authority

Finnigan, Judy (not Finnegan) and Richard Madeley, chat-show hosts

fiord (not fjord)

firearms do not confuse bullets with shotgun cartridges (containing pellets); so a gunshot wound is markedly different from a bullet wound

fire brigade l/c in general context, but cap specifics, eg, Kent Fire Brigade

firefight (or fire-fight) should not be used as a synonym of military skirmish or exchange of fire; **firefighters** try to extinguish flames. Note that we should always refer to firefighters rather than firemen, as a substantial number in the Fire Service are now women

firm do not use as a synonym of company. *See* companies

first serves as an adverb; avoid *firstly*. If a list of priorities is essential in a story, write *first*, *secondly*, *thirdly* etc. Never say *first-ever*. *See* ever, superlatives, universal claims

first aid (noun, no hyphen); but hyphenate when adjectival, eg, first-aid qualifications

First Lady caps, and restrict use primarily to US context – never for the British Prime Minister's wife

First World War (not World War One); similarly, Second World War. *See* wars

Fischer, Joschka, German politician

Fitzgerald, Garret

Five Nations Championship (rugby), initial caps, became the **Six Nations Championship** in 2000 (England, Wales, Scotland, Ireland, France and Italy)

flair, as in talent, must never be confused with **flare**, as in fire, fashion etc

flat-owners (hyphen), but **homeowners**

flaunt means to make an ostentatious or defiant display, eg, "she flaunted her finery"; to **flout** is to show contempt for, eg, "he flouted the law"

fledgeling

fleur-de-lys (not lis)

flight numbers cap in stories where the number of the flight is relevant, eg, Flight 103 (in the Lockerbie disaster)

flight path (two words)

floodlighting, but floodlit

flotation (shares), but **floatation** (tanks)

flout. *See* flaunt

flowerbed (one word); also **flowerpot**

flu (no apostrophe), acceptable for influenza

Flushing Meadows (not Meadow), New York home of the US Open tennis championships. *See* Sports special section (page 160)

Flying Squad cap, as it is the only one in the UK. But l/c fraud squads as there are several; similarly vice squads, drug squads, crime squads, regional crime squads

focused

foetus, foetal (not fetus etc); similarly, **foetid** (not fetid)

folk-song, folk-singer (use hyphen)

following avoid as a sloppy synonym of *after*. *Always* use *after* in preference

Food and Drug Administration (US)

foodstuffs where place names form part of the phrase, generally use the cap, eg, Brussels sprouts, Cheddar cheese, chicken Kiev, Cornish pasties, potatoes Lyonnaise; but keep l/c for hamburger, frankfurter etc. *See* metric

foolproof (no hyphen)

foot-and-mouth disease

for-, fore- the general rule is that the "e" is added only when the prefix has the meaning of *before*. Thus **forbears** (refrains), **forebears** (ancestors); **forgo** (go without), **forego** (go before, as in foregone conclusion). Take particular care with **forswear** and **foresee(able)**, both frequently misspelt

Forces say the Armed Forces wherever possible, but if the word has to be used alone, cap Forces both as a noun and adjectivally (as Service); but confine this formula to UK Forces, not foreign. *See* Armed Forces special section (page 14)

Foreign and Commonwealth Office usually shorten to Foreign Office or FCO (abbreviation permissible in headlines); no longer use FO

foreign appellations *The Times* uses local honorifics for:
- **France**: M, Mme, Mlle and Me (for Maître, legal)
- **Germany** and **Austria**: Herr, Frau, Fräulein
- **Spain** and Spanish-speaking **Latin America**: Señor, Señora, Señorita
- **Italy**: Signor, Signora, Signorina
- **Portugal and Brazil**: Senhor, Senhora (but not Senhorina).

Note that with Belgium, Luxembourg, Switzerland and Canada, Mr, Mrs, Miss, Ms etc are used because of those countries' linguistic sensitivities (eg, Jacques Santer, former President of the European Commission, should subsequently be Mr Santer). Similarly the English forms with Francophone Africa, where French is more the language of the elite rather than the lingua franca.

For all other nationalities, use English except where it is possible to use a local title (eg, Ayatollah, Begum, Chief, Pandit, Sheikh), or a military one (eg, Colonel Gaddafi); occasionally, where titles are in general use (eg, Baron von X in Germany), we would respect such exceptions.

NB, in **Burma**, U means Mr, Daw means Mrs; in **China**, use the first Chinese name as surname, eg, Deng Xiaoping becomes Mr Deng

foreign places as a general rule, use the spellings in *The Times Atlas of the World*, including Chinese place names (*see* Chinese names). However, *The Times* retains the Anglicised spellings of many familiar (and especially European) cities and countries, such as Brussels, Cologne, Cracow, Dunkirk, Florence, Geneva, Gothenburg, The Hague, Lyons, Majorca, Marseilles, Mexico City, Minorca, Moscow, Munich, Naples, Prague, Rheims, Rome, Salonika, Venice. *See also* Spanish regions

foreign words write in roman when foreign words and phrases have become essentially a part of the English language (eg, an elite, a debacle, a fête); otherwise, use italic (eg, a *bon mot*, a *bête noire*, the *raison d'être*). Avoid pretension by using an English phrase wherever one will serve. *See* accents

forensic means pertaining to the courts. A forensic expert could be a solicitor or a biochemist; make your meaning clear by writing *forensic scientist*, *forensic medicine* etc

for ever means always; **forever** means continuously

forklift truck

Formica (cap, proprietary)

formula plural usually formulas, but formulae in mathematical contexts

for real avoid this cliché when all you mean is "really". *See* free

Fortnum & Mason (note ampersand)

fortuitous does not mean *fortunate*. It means *by chance* or *accidental*. Do not confuse

forum plural forums. *See* referendum

four-letter words avoid wherever possible as these obscenities upset most readers. If there is no alternative (eg, in direct quotes, where they are essential to the story), soften them with asterisks – f★★★, f★★★ing, c★★★ etc. *See* obscenities

Fourth of July, or US Independence Day (not 4th)

foxhunt, foxhunting (no hyphens), as **foxhound, foxhole, master of foxhounds** (l/c). *See* hunting

FPDSavills (estate agents) – no spaces

fractions do not mix fractions and decimals in the same story. Compounds such as half-hour, half-dozen etc take a hyphen; half an hour, half a dozen do not. Hyphenate when fractions are adjectival – "two-thirds full" – but not as nouns – "two thirds of the bus was empty". *See* two thirds

franc l/c, and abbreviate as Fr40; specify if not French, eg, BFr40 (Belgian), SwFr40 (Swiss) – now often historical contexts

franchisor (no longer franchiser)

Frankenstein foods never use this pejorative phrase to describe genetically modified (GM) foods, except in direct quotations

fraud squad (l/c). *See* Flying Squad

free avoid the modern cliché *for free* when the meaning is simply *free*

"freebie" permissible as colloquialism for a handout, free trip etc, but use inverted commas

Free Churches, Free Churchman etc (caps)

freefall (one word)

Freemasonry, Mason, Masonic

French names prefer the more Anglicised style for street names etc: Rue Royale, Place de la Victoire, Boulevard des Montagnes. No need to hyphenate place names such as St Malo, St Etienne etc

french windows (l/c)

frescoes (not frescos)

Fresh Start, the Government's education initiative. Initial caps, as with other government programmes such as Third Way, Welfare to Work etc

Freud, Lucian (not Lucien)

Fringe, the Edinburgh; always cap, whether as noun or adjective (eg, a Fringe puppet show on the Royal Mile)

Frisbee (cap, proprietary)

front bench, the (noun); but **frontbencher, frontbench** power etc. *See* Politics special section (page 131)

frontline (adjective, as in the frontline states), but **the front line** (noun)

front-runner

FTSE 100 index (no longer hyphenate FT-SE); also **FTSE all-share index**; both can be shortened to the FTSE 100 or the FTSE all-share

fuchsia

fuel is becoming a greatly overworked verb, especially in headlines; always seek alternatives such as raise, increase, add to, even boost

Führer (not Fuehrer)

Fujiyama or **Mount Fuji**, not Mount Fujiyama

fulfil, but **fulfilled, fulfilling**

full points note thin space after initials and points, eg, F. W. de Klerk. But with companies, omit the full points, eg, W H Smith. *See* companies, initials

-ful, -fuls so cupfuls, not cupsful

full-time (adj), but **full time** (noun, as in football)

fulsome be very careful – and sparing – with the use of this word. It means excessive or insincere (the cliché *fulsome praise* actually means excessive praise, not generous or warm praise). Try to avoid it, especially the clichéd (and wrong) use

fundholders (as in NHS)

fundraising, fundraiser (no hyphen)

further. *See* farther

fusillade

G

Gaddafi, Colonel (Muammar), the Libyan leader

gaff is a hook or spar; **gaffe** is a blunder or indiscretion. Note to *blow the gaff* (let out a secret)

Gambia, The always use the cap definite article

gambit is a technical term in chess, meaning an opening involving a sacrifice in return for general advantage. Thus *opening gambit* is tautology. Take care with its use as a metaphor, and use sparingly

game show, as **chat show**, **quiz show**, **talk show** etc (no hyphens)

Gandhi, Mahatma, Indira etc (*never* Ghandi)

Garda. *See* Ireland

Gardeners' Question Time, not Gardener's

gas, gases (noun); **gassed, gassing** (verbal use), and note **gases** (not gasses) for present tense, eg, *doctor gases patient*

gasfield, as coalfield, oilfield

Gatt, the General Agreement on Tariffs and Trade. Its successor body is now the World Trade Organisation (WTO). *See* Uruguay Round, World Trade Organisation

Gatwick sufficiently well-known not to need airport in title. *See* airports, Heathrow

gauge (not guage)

Gaultier, Jean Paul (no hyphen)

gay now fully acceptable as a synonym for homosexual or lesbian. *See* straight

GCSE. *See* examinations

GDP, gross domestic product

GEC Alsthom became simply Alstom (note no "h") in mid-1998

gelatine (rather than gelatin)

Geldof, Bob do not write Sir Bob Geldof, as he is an honorary KBE

gender is a term of grammar; try not to use as a synonym of a person's sex

general election *always* l/c

General Secretary of the TUC (caps), but general secretary of individual unions keep l/c. *See* TUC

General Strike (of 1926) (caps)

General Synod (of the Church of England), thereafter the synod. *See* Churches special section (page 37)

Gentile(s) (cap)

gentlemen's club (prefer to

gentleman's); also **gentlemen's agreement**

George, Sir Edward (not Sir Eddie), Governor of the Bank of England

geriatric does not mean *elderly*, but is applied to medical treatment for the elderly, eg, geriatric hospital. Never use as a term of abuse

German Bight, as in shipping forecast (not Bite)

Germany full title is the Federal Republic of Germany. If referring to the area that was East Germany, say eastern Germany or the former East Germany; similarly, western Germany or the former West Germany. Ossis, Wessis permissible vernacular for inhabitants of the two parts. When plural, eg, the two Germanys, use this form, not Germanies

gerrymander

get, got usually a lazy verb for which an alternative should be sought

Getty, Sir Paul (do not use John or J. in his name)

Ghanaian (not Ghanian)

ghetto use only in the sense of an area of enforced or customary segregation, not as an ethnic neighbourhood, eg, middle-class *district*, not *ghetto*. Note plural ghettos

giant-killer, giant-killing

gibe means taunt or sneer; **gybe** means to shift direction or change course, particularly in sailing. For the sake of clarity, jibe (a variant of both) should not be used

Gibraltar (never Gibralter); and note Strait of Gibraltar (not Straits)

gig is now acceptable for a musical event, as **rave**

gillie (rather than ghillie)

gipsy. *See* gypsy

girl do not use as a synonym of *woman*

girlfriend (one word, as boyfriend). Use girlfriend only for young people; otherwise woman friend or just friend (where the gender is obvious)

girlie (not girly)

giro (l/c), as in benefit payments, cheques etc

Giscard d'Estaing, Valéry; thereafter M Giscard

giveaway (noun or adjective), one word, as takeaway; but to give away

glamorise, glamorous, but **glamour**

glasnost (not italic)

glassmaker

GlaxoSmithKline, the merged pharmaceuticals company (GSK for short)

Glen Coe, the valley; but **Glencoe** for the battle, the village and the pass

Glorious Twelfth, the (caps)

GMB say the GMB general union

Go, the no-frills airline, with an initial cap

gobbledegook

God cap when referring to just one, in any religion. He, His, Him also take cap. Many gods, use l/c, as in *the Greek gods*. *See* Christian terms, and Churches special section (page 37)

godforsaken, **godless** (l/c), but **God-fearing**

godparents, **godfather**, **godmother**, **godson**, **goddaughter**, **godchild**

Goebbels, Joseph (not Goebells etc)

goer as a suffix, run on as one word, as in **churchgoer**, **partygoer**, **theatregoer** etc

go-kart (use hyphen)

Goldeneye (the James Bond film, not GoldenEye)

Golden Jubilee caps for the Queen's celebration in 2002, l/c in general context

Golders Green (no apostrophe)

goldmine, **goldmining**

Goldsmiths College, London (no apostrophe). Goldsmiths has a Warden, not a Rector. *See* London University

goodbye

goodwill one word, whether used as a noun or adjective

Gorazde in Bosnia (not Goradze)

Gorbachev, Mikhail

gorilla

Gormley, Antony (the sculptor)

Gothenburg (not Göteborg)

Gothic (cap), rather than *Gothick*

Government cap all governments, British and overseas, when referring to a specific one, eg, "the Government resigned last night", "the Argentine Government sent troops", and specific past administrations such as "the Heath Government"; only l/c when unspecific or one that has yet to be formed, eg, "all the governments since the war", or "the next Tory/Labour government would raise pensions".

Also l/c government in all adjectival contexts, eg, a government minister, a government decision, government expenditure. A further instance of l/c use is in phrases such as "the Bosnian government troops" or "the British government-backed trade delegation", when the use is again principally adjectival.

Also, note that provincial or state governments in Australia, Canada, India etc retain the l/c. *See* Politics special section (page 131)

government departments cap both when giving full title (eg, Department of Trade and Industry), and even when abbreviated, as in Health Department, Education Department, Trade Department etc. The same applies to ministries, home and overseas. *See* departments

Government Information and Communication Service (initial caps) can be shortened to government information service (l/c) or GICS. It comprises the information officers in government departments

Governor of the Bank of England (cap at every mention), also cap Deputy Governor of the Bank. Also, cap the Governor of the Falkland Islands at every mention; but cap prison governors at first mention only, eg, James X, Governor of Parkhurst, thereafter l/c, and l/c deputy governors of prisons

Graces *The Three Graces* (Canova's statue). *See* Arts special section (page 18)

Grade II listed, Grade II★ listed etc

gram, not gramme; similarly, kilogram. *See* metric

grandad, but **granddaughter**

Grand Jury (caps) in US contexts

grandmaster (chess) l/c. *See* chess names

Grappelli, Stéphane (use acute accent)

grassroots (adjective), the **grass roots** (noun). Still a cliché and should be used sparingly

great and the good, the (all l/c, and quotes usually unnecessary)

Greater London Authority (GLA at subsequent mention) is the strategic government for London, consisting of the Mayor of London and the London Assembly, backed up by a staff of some 400. The **London Assembly** (*not* the Greater London Assembly) is an elected body of 25 members providing checks and balances on the Mayor of London

greater or lesser degree *lesser* is not correct but is common usage

Great Ormond Street Hospital for Children (no longer Sick Children)

Greco-, not Graeco–

green belt (l/c), but greenfield sites (similarly brownfield)

Green Paper (caps). *See also* White Paper

Green Party, or the Greens, but **green issues** etc

grisly means horrifying, repugnant; **grizzly** means greyish, grizzled, or is a short form of grizzly bear

grottoes

ground(s) in the sense of reason, do not use plural unless more than one is given; eg, "he gave up his job on the ground of illness"; but "he gave up his job on the grounds of his failed marriage and illness"

Group 4 (security company)

G-string

Guantanamo Bay, Cuba (no accents). *See* War on Terror

guerrilla beware of loaded terms for advocates of political violence. *See* terrorist

guest avoid using as a verb (Lady X will guest on the show; say Lady X will be among the guests, or Lady X is a guest). *See* host

guesthouse (no hyphen)

guldebook similarly, **chequebook, formbook, stylebook, textbook** etc

Guides (not Girl Guides); Girlguiding UK is the new name (April 2002) for the Guide Association; the individual members are still known as Guides, Brownies and Rainbows. *See* Scouts

Guildhall (London); never *the* Guildhall

guinea-pig (hyphen)

Guinness note *The Guinness Book of Records* has *The* as part of the title

Gujarati, person or language (not Guje-)

Gulf, the avoid the term Persian Gulf as it angers Iraqis and many other Arabs

gunboat, gunfight, gunfire, gunman, gunpoint, gunshot, gunsmith but **gun dog**

gunned down avoid this Americanism; instead say *shot dead*

gunwales (nautical, not gunwhales)

Gurkhas

guttural (not gutteral)

Guyana (formerly British Guiana, now independent); do not confuse with **French Guiana** (still a French overseas territory). The adjective from Guyana is Guyanese, also the person

Gwyn, Nell

Gypsy/gypsy (not gipsy). Use the cap when referring to a specific group of this semi-nomadic people, but l/c in the fashion or general sense, as in "gypsy style is the look for spring". The other wandering groups in Britain are the Irish tinkers, who prefer the name **Irish travellers**; the **Scottish Gypsies/ travellers**; and the hippies, whom we call **New Age travellers**; **travellers** is a useful generic term. Note (the) **Roma** is the term for Gypsies from the Continent, some of whom have sought asylum in Western Europe. The singular and adjectival form is **Romany**, eg, a Romany woman, but Gypsy can be used in the same way. Note also that the Gypsy Council (or Romani Kris) is not the same as the Gypsy Council for Education, Culture, Welfare and Civil Rights (GCECWCR). This second organisation must not be shortened to Gypsy Council

H

Häagen-Dazs the ice-cream invented in America

Haberdashers' Aske's School, Elstree and Lewisham

Habsburg (not Hapsburg)

haemorrhage means heavy and potentially dangerous bleeding, not simply bleeding. Beware of misuse in metaphor

Hague, Ffion

Hague, The

hairdresser, hairdressing, hairbrush, haircut, hairdryer, hairpin, hairstyle

Haiti, Haitian note that Haiti must never be described as an island; it is joined to the Dominican Republic and together they constitute the island of Hispaniola

haj pilgrimage to Mecca (l/c and roman)

haka the Maori war-dance (l/c and roman)

half-mast (hyphenate)

half-time in a football match etc; the half time in business context (but half-time results)

halfway (no hyphen), but **half-hearted**

Halley's comet. *See* heavenly bodies

handheld (computers etc), as desktop, laptop, palmtop etc

Hallowe'en

handmade, handbuilt (no hyphen)

handout (as a noun, no hyphen)

hangar (aircraft), **hanger** (clothes)

hanged "The murderer was hanged at dawn" – never *hung*. Clothes are hung on a washing line or a hanger

Hansard

harass, harassment

hardcore (one word as adjective, eg, hardcore pornography); but the hard core of the rebels (two words as noun); similarly, hard core (rubble)

hardline (adjective), but *taking a hard line*

Haringey is a London borough and council, **Harringay** a London neighbourhood

Harley-Davidson (hyphenate)

HarperCollins, or **HarperCollins Publishers**, is owned by The News Corporation. *See* News International

Harpers & Queen

Harrods (no apostrophe). *See* Al Fayed

harvest festival (l/c)

Hattersley, Lord (*not* "of Sparkbrook")

Havisham, Miss (not Miss Haversham) in Dickens's *Great Expectations*

Hawaiian

hay fever (no hyphen)

headache avoid as a synonym of *difficulty*

head-butt (noun or verb)

headcount (no hyphen)

headhunt, headhunting etc (no hyphens)

headlines avoid the worst clichés and hyperboles such as *bash, crash, shock, slam* etc; but words such as *bid* (for attempt), *crisis, hit* (adversely affect), *row* (clash or dispute) – all of which should appear only sparingly in text – are permissible in headlines, **provided they are not overworked**.

Inverted commas must always be single in headlines, straps and display panels on News, Sport and Business pages. *See* quotation marks

headmaster, headmistress one word and l/c except in the formal, official title (and then cap at first mention only). Some schools have variants on the usual style; Eton, Harrow, Rugby and Westminster have a Head Master; St Paul's School and Manchester Grammar School have a High Master; King Edward's School, Birmingham, has a Chief Master; Dulwich, Haileybury and Marlborough have a Master. The correct form is given in the *Independent Schools Year Book*. Use the colloquial head only in headlines; and note that **head teacher** is two words except when part of the designated title

headroom (one word), as elbowroom, legroom

heads of state when these are royals, such as King Abdullah of Jordan, after the first mention refer to them as the King (cap). The cap at subsequent mentions applies only to overseas heads of state and the British Royal Family; ie, Prince B. of Thailand (a minor royal) would become the prince thereafter. *See* Royal Family, titles

head up (an organisation etc) avoid; write simply, eg, "she will head the organisation"

healthcare (one word)

heartbroken, heartbreaking, heartfelt, heartstrings, but hyphenate **heart-rending, heart-throb**

Heathrow sufficiently well-known not to need airport in title. *See* airports, Gatwick

Heaven, Hell cap in religious context only. *See* Devil

heavenly bodies cap the proper names of planets, stars, constellations etc: Venus, Arcturus, the Plough, Aries; for comets, l/c the word comet in, for example, Halley's comet. The Sun, the Moon, the Earth, the Universe are capped in their planetary or astronomical sense (*see* Earth). Use l/c for the adjectives lunar and solar, but cap Martian both adjectivally and as a noun

Heep, Uriah (not Heap)

Hell's Angels

help to (plus verb), eg, "he helped **to** make the cake" (not "he helped make the cake")

helping the police with their inquiries avoid this phrase – suspects rarely willingly help the police. Say "were being interviewed" instead

helpline (one word). *See* hotline

hemisphere northern, southern, eastern, western

heraldry do not confuse **crests** with **coats of arms**. Most arms consist of a shield and a crest; crests are the topmost part of the coat of arms (think of the crest of a bird or a wave)

Hereford and Worcester abolished on April 1, 1998. It has been replaced by a new

Worcestershire County Council and a new unitary authority for Herefordshire. *See* unitary authorities

Heriot-Watt University, Edinburgh

Her Majesty's pleasure (detained at)

Herzegovina (as in Bosnia-Herzegovina), not Hercegovina. *See* Yugoslav

Heyhoe Flint, Rachael (no hyphen, not Rachel)

Hezbollah (Party of God) in Iran and Lebanon; soft-hyphenate (on a break) as Hezb-ollah

Hibernian means of or concerning Ireland, *not* Scotland – despite the Edinburgh football club of that name

hiccup (not hiccough)

hi-fi is an acceptable abbreviation (noun or adjective) of high fidelity

high acceptable usage as a noun, eg, "she was on a high". But avoid clichés such as *all-time high* and *hits new high*

highbrow, lowbrow

high command avoid its clichéd use, as in "Tory high command". *See* Politics special section (page 131)

High Commissioner (with caps) when specific, eg, the Indian High Commissioner; thereafter, the high commissioner. Remember that

Commonwealth countries and the UK have high commissioners serving in high commissions in each other's countries, not ambassadors serving in embassies. *See* Ambassador

High Court. *See* Courts special section (page 47)

highfalutin

high-flyer

High Sheriff (caps) when specific

high street is l/c and no hyphen in general sense, as in high street prices. But cap in specifics, eg, Putney High Street

high-tech (adjective); spell out in text, but hi-tech is acceptable in headlines

hike never use in the American sense of *a rise* or *to raise* (rates etc); permissible only in direct quotes, or in the context of walking (hitch-hike etc)

Hinckley, Leicestershire; but **Hinkley Point**, Somerset

Hindi for language context (the Hindi language); but use **Hindu** for religious or ethnic contexts (an adherent to Hinduism, or relating to Hinduism)

hippy, **hippies** nowadays as old-fashioned as beatniks. *See* Gypsy, travellers

Hirst, Damien (not Damian), the artist

historic, **historical** prefer *an historic event* rather than *a historic*. *See* a, an. Also, take care with use of *historical* and *historic*; the former can refer only to past history, while the latter can refer to a contemporary event likely to be of long-term significance. But *an historic building* is now in common usage as a synonym of an old building

hit avoid in text in sense of *affected*, eg, "Homeowners were hit last night by an interest rate rise", or in the sense of attack, eg, "The minister hit out at his critics". Sparing use of the verb in headlines is permissible

hitch-hiker, **hitch-hiking** etc

Hitchin, Hertfordshire (not Hitchen)

hitlist, hitman (no hyphens)

HIV is a virus, *not* a disease. Do not write *HIV virus* (tautology), but use a phrase such as *HIV-infected*. *See* Aids

hoards are stocks or stores (of treasure, for example); to hoard is to amass and store food, money etc; **hordes** are large groups or gangs (of wild beasts etc)

Hogmanay (cap)

hoi polloi do not use "the" (it means, literally, "the many"). Roman, not italic

holidaymaker (one word)

Holland now use the Netherlands (no longer cap The) for all contexts except sports teams, historical uses, or when referring to the provinces of North and South Holland. The adjective is Dutch. *See* Netherlands

Holy Communion (caps). *See* Christian terms

Holy Grail (caps)

Holyroodhouse. *See* Palace

homebuyers, **homeowners** (no hyphens)

Home Counties, the (caps)

home-made (hyphenate)

home town (two words), but hyphenate in adjectival use, eg, home-town memories

homoeopathy (not the American homeopathy)

homogeneous means having parts all of the same kind; **homogenous** means similar owing to common descent

Homo sapiens. *See* scientific names

homosexual. *See* gay

Hon, the normally use this form of address (the Hon So-and-So) only on the Court Page

Hong Kong, but Hongkong and Shanghai Banking Corporation (HSBC). Until July 1, 1997, when Britain handed the colony over to China, Hong Kong had a Governor (cap). *See* Midland

honours people are **appointed Privy Counsellor**, **Baronet**, **KBE**, **CBE**, **OBE**, **MBE** etc; never say they were made, received, were awarded, or got the OBE etc. **Peers** and above (viscounts etc) are **created**, not appointed etc. At investitures, those honoured receive the insignia of the award, not the award itself. Normally (except on Court Page) omit honours and decorations after names, but the following can be used where relevant; KG, KT, VC, GC, OM, CH, MP, QC, RA, FRS etc. *See* Titles special section (page 171)

honours lists. *See* New Year Honours

Hoon, Geoff (prefer to Geoffrey)

Hoover is a trade name so must be capped as a noun; generally, use **vacuum cleaner**, or to **vacuum**. But as a verb use l/c, eg, he hoovered up his food

hopefully try to avoid in the sense of *it is hoped that*, even though this usage is so widespread

Horse Guards Parade

horse race/racing two words, but *racing* alone is preferable. Note **Horserace Betting Levy Board**. *See* racecourse, Sports special section (page 160)

horticulturist (not horticulturalist)

hospitalise, hospitalisation
always avoid these Americanisms;
say *taken to hospital* etc

host avoid using as a verb as in
"Arsenal will host Aston Villa on
Saturday"; use **play host to** instead.
But a person can host an event

hotline (one word); similarly,
helpline

hotpants (one word)

hot-water bottle (note hyphen)

hoummos. *See* taramasalata

housebuilder, housebuilding; but
note the **House Builders
Federation** (no longer
House-Builders')

however when used in the sense of
nevertheless, always needs a comma
after it (and before, when in the
middle of a sentence, eg, "It was said,
however, that the agent …")

Hubble Space Telescope (caps)

Hudson Bay, but Hudson's Bay
Company

human beings, rather than just
humans, at first mention

Human Genome Project (caps)

human rights European
Convention on Human Rights;
European Court of Human Rights;
both operate under the aegis of the
Council of Europe, not the
European Union (or EC). *See* Courts
special section (page 47)

humorist (not humourist)

Humphrys, John (radio and TV);
but **Barry Humphries** (Dame
Edna Everage etc)

hunting with hounds (not with
dogs). *See* foxhunt

Hussein, the late King (of
Jordan), not *Husain*; similarly,
President Saddam Hussein (of
Iraq)

Hutus, Tutsis, the plural of the
Rwandan tribes (not simply Hutu,
Tutsi)

hydroelectric (no hyphen)

hyphens generally be sparing with
hyphens and run together words
where the sense suggests and where
they look familiar and right; eg,
**blacklist, businessman,
goldmine, knockout,
intercontinental, motorcycle,
takeover** and **walkover**. Unusual
hyphenations will be listed separately
in this Style Guide. However, a few
guidelines can be specified:

a. usually run together prefixes
except where the last letter of the
prefix is the same as the first letter
of the word to which it attaches:
**prearrange, postwar, prewar,
nonconformist** ; but **pre-empt,
co-ordinate, co-operate,
re-establish**

b. hyphenate generally in composites
where the same two letters come
together, eg, **film-makers**, but an

exception should be made for double "r" in the middle: **override**, **overrule** (not over-ride etc), and note **granddaughter** and **goddaughter**

c. generally do not use dangling hyphens – say *full and part-time employment* etc; but this does not apply to prefixes – pre- or post-match drinks

d. for hyphenation when qualifying adjectives, *see* adverbs

e. always use a hyphen rather than a slash (/) in dates etc – 1982-83 (not 1982/83)

hyperthermia too hot; **hypothermia** too cold

I

IATA (all caps), the International Air Transport Association

ice-cap (use hyphen)

ice-cream (hyphen), similarly **ice-lolly**. *See* Häagen-Dazs

Identikit is proprietary, so cap; but **photofit** l/c

, ie, use comma either side. *See* eg

IF (not If), short for Intelligent Finance, the internet and telephone banking arm of the Halifax

ill-health (hyphen); similarly **ill-feeling**, **ill-intentioned** etc

iMac (l/c and cap) computers

IMAX (all caps) cinemas

Immigration Service (caps, as Prison Service, Probation Service)

impacted on avoid this Americanism

Imperial War Museum North (use only this style) is in Trafford, which is a metropolitan borough within Greater Manchester. Do not locate it simply as in Manchester

imply. *See* infer

impostor (not imposter)

impresario

Impressionist, Post-Impressionist. *See* artistic movements

in addition to prefer *as well as* or *besides*

inadmissible (not -able)

include do not confuse with *comprise*; "breakfast includes toast and coffee", but "breakfast comprises cereals, toast, butter, marmalade and coffee" (ie, where the full list of elements is given)

incommunicado

Independent Schools Council information service (ISCis) is the new name for ISIS (the Independent Schools Information Service)

indestructible (not -able)

index plural is indices, but indexes for books

Indian place names continue to use Bombay rather than Mumbai, Madras rather than Chennai, Calcutta rather than Kolkata, and Delhi rather than New Delhi, except where the new names form part of an official company name or similar title. If in doubt, put the alternative name in brackets

indispensable (not -ible)

Indo-China

Industrial Revolution, the (caps)

industrial tribunals have now been renamed employment tribunals. They end with a **judgment** or a **decision**, *not* a verdict. Only juries in court hearings, or magistrates hearing cases summarily, deliver a verdict. Note that **immigration adjudicators** and **immigration appeal tribunals** deliver **determinations**. *See* Courts special section (page 47)

inevitable do not use as a synonym of *customary, usual* or *predictable*

in fact can almost invariably be omitted

infer do not confuse with *imply*; to *infer* is to draw a conclusion from a suggestion, to *imply* is to make the suggestion. A quick mnemonic: we **imply** things when we speak, we **infer** things when we listen

infighting (one word), but **in-house** and **in-flight** (both with hyphen)

infra-red

initials where totally familiar, no need to spell out at first mention (eg, BBC, TUC, Nato etc). Otherwise, usually give name in full followed by initials in parentheses, and the abbreviated form thereafter (though sometimes a word such as "the organisation" or "the group" will be preferable to avoid a mass of initials

in the same story). Also, with a body as well known as the UN, it would be absurd to write the United Nations (UN), so use discretion.

Where the initials can be spoken as a word, we normally write them as upper and lower case, eg, Nato, Gatt, Unesco, Eta – but there are some important exceptions to this, eg, MORI, IATA, RADA, RIBA, SANE, BUPA and AXA.

With people's names, put points between the initials (with thin space between), though omit points in names of companies such as W H Smith, J Sainsbury

injure, injury implies something more serious than *hurt*. Do not normally say someone received an injury – prefer to say they suffered or sustained an injury, or (simply) were injured. Injured or sick people should not be described as *satisfactory* or *critical* – it is their condition that is satisfactory etc

Inland Revenue subsequent mentions, the Revenue (cap). *See* taxman

innocent take great care with this word, and avoid phrases such as "the innocent victim of the attack" and clichés such as "innocent children". Best to stick to its literal sense of not guilty

innocuous

Inns of Court the order of precedence among the Inns is

Lincoln's Inn, Inner Temple, Middle Temple, Gray's Inn

inoculate

inpatients, **outpatients** (no hyphen)

inquests. *See* coroner's court

inquire, inquiry *not* enquire, enquiry. But note the exception, Directory Enquiries

insignia, plural. *See* honours

in so far as use the four words in this expression; insofar is the American version

install, but **instalment**

instil

Institute of Contemporary Arts ("of" not "for" and plural Arts)

Institute of Directors IoD acceptable for headings and occasionally in text, though prefer *the institute* after first mention in full

insure you **insure** against risk; you **assure** your life; **ensure** means to make certain

Intelligence cap as a noun in the context of the security services, eg, "he was in British Intelligence", but l/c in non-specific contexts, eg, "she provided useful intelligence to MI6"; also l/c for adjectival uses, eg, "she was interviewed by intelligence officers"

intelligentsia

intensive do not confuse with *intense* or *extreme*. It means concentrated, as in *intensive care*

InterCity no longer exists as a rail company so use this form only in historic contexts. Write **inter-city** as the generic. *See* train companies

interdependence

interesting avoid as an adjective in text; let the reader decide

interest rate cuts/rises (no hyphens); never use *hikes* for *rises*

interfaith

International Atomic Energy Agency (IAEA) *never* Authority

International Olympic Committee (not Olympics), IOC as abbreviation. *See* Olympics

International Space Station (initial caps)

Internazionale, the Milan football club; now call it Inter Milan at first mention, thereafter Inter. The other big club in the city is AC Milan (shortened to AC thereafter)

internet, the now l/c, also the **net**; similarly the **web**, **website**. *See* world wide web

interpretative (not interpretive)

interred = buried; **interned** = imprisoned. Do not confuse

intifada (religious struggle or uprising), l/c and roman

Inuit prefer to Eskimo. *See* Eskimo

inverted commas should be used as sparingly as possible in text: eg, unnecessary in constructions such as he *described the book as "turgid"*. They are no longer to be used with works of art. *See also* italics, quotation marks

Iran, not Persia (though Persia in historical context). The language is not Iranian or Persian; it is Farsi

irascible (not irrascible)

Ireland the two parts should be called the Republic of Ireland or the Irish Republic (avoid Eire except in direct quotes or historical context), and Northern Ireland or Ulster. Do not use the phrase the Six Counties. Other important styles:

a. loyalist with a l/c "l" (and no quotes) – to balance republican and nationalist

b. Unionist, Unionism (caps)

c. the North, the South (caps in this specific Irish context)

d. the Republic (likewise), the Province

e. the Troubles

f. the Garda (the police force; but garda/gardai for policeman/ policemen); but the phrase Irish police is acceptable

g. Londonderry, but Derry City Council; and Derry when in direct quotes or in a specifically republican context (this latter rarely)

h. Belfast: cap North Belfast and South Belfast as well as East and West Belfast; and note Shankill Road (not Shankhill)

i. Downing Street declaration

j. Anglo-Irish agreement

k. *Frameworks for the Future*, or the framework document (l/c) – the Anglo-Irish proposals of February 1995

l. Northern Ireland Assembly; cap Assembly now it has become an established body; same cap rules apply as to Parliament. Similarly Northern Ireland Executive (in context of the Government)

m. avoid Provos as synonym of the Provisional IRA, except in quotes

n. the Taoiseach is an acceptable alternative for Irish Prime Minister

o. Irish counties should be written as Co Donegal, Co Down etc. *See* counties

p. Orange Order, Orangemen (caps)

iridescent (not irr-)

Iron Curtain

ironic beware of misuse. It means using or displaying irony, or in the nature of irony; it does not mean strange or paradoxical

irreconcilable

irredeemable means not able to be redeemed, saved or reformed; do not confuse with **irremediable**, which means not able to be remedied, incurable, or irreparable

irresistible (not -able)

Isa(s) individual savings account(s) (l/c), as with Tessas and Peps. Hyphenate mini-Isas, maxi-Isas

Isaf, the International Security Assistance Force (in Afghanistan); not Security *and* Assistance. *See* War on Terror

-ise, -isation avoid the z construction in almost all cases, eg, apologise, organise, emphasise, televise. But note capsize, synthesizer

Islam is the religion of the Muslims. Islamic is interchangeable with Muslim as the adjective, though normally use Islamic with religion and fundamentalism, Muslim with architecture, politics etc

Israeli is a native of Israel; Israelite refers to Ancient Israel

italics avoid in headlines and be as restrained as possible in their use in text. However, certain areas do always take italics:

a. all works of art, even where quotation marks used to be used;

thus, italics for titles of books, long and short poems, short stories, newspapers (*see* separate list under newspapers), magazines, pamphlets, chapter headings, White Papers, Green Papers, official reports and studies, programmes on radio and television, films, plays, computer games, musical works including operas, songs, hymns, album titles etc (*see* musical vocabulary), paintings, drawings, sculptures, titles of exhibitions. *See* Arts special section (page 18)

b. less common, non-Anglicised foreign words go in italics, but err on the side of roman (eg, in extremis, hors d'oeuvre, angst). *See* foreign words

c. names of ships, aircraft, locomotives, spacecraft etc

d. a word may be italicised for emphasis, but again be sparing with this device

ITN never say ITN news. *See* television

ITV1 and **ITV2**, the two separate independent television channels

J

jack-knife (use hyphen)

Jacuzzi is a trade name, so cap; use whirlpool bath if in doubt

jail, jailer (not gaol, gaoler)

jargon like journalese and slang, to be strictly avoided; specialised areas always need explanations for our readers

Jazz FM do not use the l/c logo version

Jedda

Jeep is proprietary, so must be capped; use only if strictly applicable, otherwise *cross-country vehicle, small military truck* etc

Jehovah's Witness(es)

Jekyll and Hyde (*The Strange Case of Dr Jekyll and Mr Hyde*, by R. L. Stevenson)

Jerusalem l/c for east/west Jerusalem

jet lag (two words)

jetliner avoid; say *airliner* or simply *jet*

jet ski two words as noun, but to *jet-ski* (verb, hyphen)

jeweller, jewellery

jibe avoid this spelling. *See* gibe

jihad, holy war (roman, l/c)

JobCentre initial cap and also cap "C" in the middle

jobseeker's allowance

job titles the general rule is that for the most senior high-profile jobs we should cap at first mention, and thereafter l/c. Thus most church titles, senior civil servants, diplomatic and political leaders, civic leaders, Editor (of well-known leading publications), Director-General (of the BBC, CBI etc), Vice-Chancellor and academic titles, Chief Constable and police ranks, military titles, President of a small number of high-profile national institutions (eg, President of the Law Society, the TUC etc), all take the cap at first mention and then – usually – l/c thereafter. Exceptions where the cap is retained are Prime Minister, President (of a state), Archbishop and Bishop.

However, chairman, director, managing director (of a company), general secretary (of a union), artistic director (of a theatre) etc are l/c; so are most presidents and chairmen of societies and institutions. A certain amount of discretion is needed in this difficult area

jodhpurs

John o' Groats (no longer use 's)

Johns Hopkins University, Baltimore

Joint Chiefs of Staff (US)

Jones, Vinnie (not Vinny), the ex-footballer, now actor

Jonsson, Ulrika

joyrider (no hyphen), but use as little as possible as the term gives offence to many readers; the last emotion these car thieves bring to their victims is joy. An alternative could be *young car thief*

JP (Justice of the Peace) acceptable alternative for non-stipendiary magistrate. *See* magistrates' courts and Courts special section (page 47)

jubilee strictly a fiftieth anniversary, though Queen Victoria had a golden and a diamond one; so the word can be used as a periodic celebration, especially of royalty. Note the Queen's **Golden Jubilee** in 2002, and also note **Jubilee Line** (caps) on the London Underground

Judaea (not Judea)

judges' names all **circuit judges and below** (ie, those in the Crown Court, in county courts, and district judges) must **always include their Christian name (or first name) at first mention**. Thus, write Judge Fred Potts at first mention, subsequently Judge Potts or simply the judge.

Christian (or first) names will not normally be necessary with High Court judges unless there are two or more with the same surname, where again it will be essential to differentiate.

The failure to identify a judge correctly can lead to complaints, corrections and even the payment of substantial damages.

In the High Court, Mr Justice X should be referred to this way throughout a story (or simply the judge) – never as Judge X. Be careful not to confuse a judge in the Court of Appeal (a Lord Justice of Appeal) with a law lord of the House of Lords, the most senior judges, who are Lords of Appeal in Ordinary (such as Lord Nolan and Lord Hoffmann).

Note designation of Lady Justice Butler-Sloss.

See Courts special section (page 47)

judging by one of the most frequently misused unrelated (or disconnected) participle constructions. Remember, the phrase must have a related subject to follow (I, we, she etc). A convenient alternative is "to judge from ..." (eg, "Judging by this film, the country is in a mess" is wrong; "To judge from this film, the country is in a mess" is correct; so is "Judging by this film, we conclude that the country is in a mess"). *See* participles

judgment (not judgement)

jukebox (no hyphen)

jump-jet (hyphen), but **jumbo jet** (no hyphen)

junior abbreviate to Jr (not Jnr) in the American context, eg, John Eisendorf Jr. *See* senior

Justices' Clerks' Society (two apostrophes)

juvenile courts no longer exist; they are now called **youth courts**. *See* Courts special section (page 47)

K

k avoid for 1,000 except in direct quotes

kaftan, but **cagoule**

Kant, Immanuel (not Emmanuel)

Karajan, Herbert von; thereafter just Karajan (not von Karajan)

Karpov, Anatoly; **Kasparov, Garry**. *See* chess names, Russian names

Kathmandu

Kellogg's Corn Flakes, but cornflakes (generic)

Kentucky Fried Chicken has been rebranded as **KFC**, so do not use the full capped version for the company or restaurant chain except in historical context. Permissible to refer to the product as Kentucky fried chicken (l/c)

kerosene is American for paraffin

Kevorkian, Dr Jack (the American euthanasia doctor; not Kervorkian)

Key Stage 1, 2, 3 etc (caps and figures for Government's educational targets)

Kfor, the Nato-led force in Kosovo (not KFOR). It is short for Kosovo Force, not Kosovo Protection Force. *See also* Kosovo

Khan Imran Khan and Jemima Khan are happy to be known as Mr Khan and Mrs Khan respectively after first mention. Imran is permissible on its own in headlines. But in most cases, beware of Khan as the family name; it is usually a title given to officials or rulers in Central Asia

Khartoum

Khashoggi, Soraya, **Adnan** etc

Khmer Rouge the name of a Cambodian faction. A Khmer is a Cambodian

Khrushchev, Nikita

kick-off (noun), but to *kick off*

kick-start (hyphenate, noun or verb)

Kiley, Bob (prefer to Robert), Commissioner of Transport for London, or Transport Commissioner for short

killer can be used for *murderer* but do not use *assassin* as a synonym

kilogram (not kilogramme). *See* gram, metric

kilometres per hour correct abbreviation is km/h rather than kph. *See* metric

kilowatt-hour correct abbreviation is kWh. The cost of generating electricity at a power station is usually expressed in pence per kilowatt-hour (2.9p/kWh). *See* megawatts

King's College London (apostrophe, no commas). *See* London University

King's Cross, London

King's Lynn, Norfolk

Kings Road, Chelsea (do not use apostrophe)

Kingston upon Hull is the official name for Hull; normally just say **Hull**. Note that Humberside no longer exists as a local authority. *See* unitary authorities

Kingston upon Thames (no hyphens); say southwest London, rather than Surrey; but note that Surrey County Council is still based in Kingston. *See* postal addresses

Kinkladze, Giorgi, footballer (not Georgi)

kitchen cabinet l/c cabinet in this informal context. *See* Cabinet

Kitemark. *See* British Standards Institution

Kit Kat (two words)

kneejerk (reaction etc), no hyphen; but beware of overuse

knockout (noun), but to *knock out*

knowhow (one word as noun)

knowledgeable

Knox-Johnston, Sir Robin (yachtsman)

Kodak is a trade name, so must be capped

Koh-i-noor diamond

Koran, the (cap and roman, like the Bible)

Korean names, unlike Chinese, take all initial caps but no hyphens, eg, Roh Tae Woo

Kosovo, Kosovan do not use Kosova, Kosovar

kowtow (no hyphen)

Ku Klux Klan (no hyphens)

KwaZulu/Natal (not Natal/ KwaZulu). *See* South Africa

Kyoto Protocol (cap P)

Kyrgyzstan (no longer Kirghizia)

L

Labor Day (in US), but keep Anglicised the Defence Department etc

Labor Party (in Australia)

Labour Party (in UK); abbreviate in lists etc to Lab. *See* Politics special section (page 131)

Ladbrokes, the betting shop, but Ladbroke plc; note also William Hill and Coral (neither takes final "s")

lady, **ladies** prefer to write *woman*, *women*

Lafite, Château. *See* wines

Lagos is not the capital of Nigeria; Abuja is

laissez faire do not use the *laisser* version

Lake District do not include *Lake* when the name contains its equivalent; thus Windermere, Derwent Water, but Lake Bassenthwaite

lambast (not lambaste)

lamé (to distinguish it from lame)

lamppost (no hyphen)

Land Rover (no hyphen); similarly Range Rover

Land's End

landmine (no hyphen)

landslide (political), **landslip** (earth)

languor, **languorous** (not -our)

lap dancer, **lap dancing** (nouns), but a lap-dancing club (adjectival, hyphenate)

laptop (computer), no hyphen. *See* desktop

largesse (not largess)

last, **past** *last* should not be used as a synonym of *latest*; "the last few days" means the final few days; "the past few days" means the most recent few days

Last Post, like Reveille, is sounded, not played

Latin be sparing in its use, apart from in the Law Report. When Latin phrases are in common usage, use roman rather than italics, eg, quid pro quo, QED, ex parte injunction, habeas corpus

Latin dancing cap Latin in this and all other contexts, whether the Latin language or history, Latin music, Latin temperament etc

latitude, **longitude** write 45° 32'N, 40° 17'W etc

La traviata (note l/c "t")

launch pad (two words)

launderette (not laundrette)

Laurence, Commodore Tim (Princess Royal's husband). No longer Captain. *See* Titles special section (page 171)

lavatory prefer to toilet (or even worse, loo)

law lords, **law officers** (l/c). *See* judges, Courts special section (page 47)

lawnmower (one word)

Law Report in *The Times*, always initial caps and singular (not Reports); so the style for x-refs is **Law Report, page 42** etc (bold, set right)

lay, **lie** a person lays a carpet (transitive verb), but lies on a carpet (intransitive). *Never* confuse

lay-by, but **layout** and **layoff**

lay waste means to devastate or destroy, so it does not need a following "to". Goats can lay waste a field, not lay waste to a field

Leader of the Commons/House of Lords; Leader of the Opposition (ie, caps); however, Labour leader (l/c), Tory leader (l/c) etc. *See* Politics special section (page 131)

lean, **leap** past tenses leant, leapt (not leaned, leaped)

Leaning Tower of Pisa (initial caps)

Lea River, but Lee Valley Regional Park Authority etc

Learjet (one word)

learnt (past tense and past participle of learn); **learned** (adjective, as in *scholarly*)

Lebanon, not the Lebanon (except occasionally in historical context). *See* Sudan

le Carré, John

Lecs (initial cap only), short for local enterprise councils. *See* Tecs

Lee Kuan Yew (of Singapore)

Left, the cap in the political context when referring to a group of like-minded individuals, eg, "The Left added to Tony Blair's worries"; but l/c in "the party swung to the left". When the Left is qualified, keep the adjective l/c, eg, the hard Left, the far Left. Also, **the left wing**, **left-wing contenders**, **leftwingers**. *See* Right

legal aid l/c and never hyphenate, even adjectivally in phrases such as legal aid cases. Note that the Legal Aid Board has been replaced by the Legal Services Commission. *See* Courts special section (page 47)

legal terms in general, use l/c for titles etc except when in full or specific; thus, the Recorder of Liverpool (thereafter the recorder), the West London Magistrate, Chelmsford Crown Court,

Horseferry Road Magistrates' Court (caps on first mention), etc; but "the court was told", "the judge said", "the magistrate ordered" etc.

The Bench is capped only when referring to the judges as a group; a bench of magistrates is always l/c. *See* magistrates' courts.

Always cap the Bar and the Inn (even when used on its own). *See* Courts special section (page 47)

legendary avoid its clichéd use

legionella, listeria, salmonella are all bacteria, not viruses

legionnaires' disease

Legion of Honour or **Légion d'honneur** either form is acceptable, according to context

legroom (one word), also elbowroom, headroom

leitmotiv (l/c, roman), prefer to leitmotif

Le Manoir aux Quat' Saisons (restaurant)

Leonardo da Vinci at second mention always Leonardo, never da Vinci

leper do not use as a metaphor or as a form of abuse

lèse-majesté (treason, or insult to a monarch) takes italic and accents

less in quantity, **fewer** in number. *See* fewer

lesser opposite to greater (eg, the

lesser evil); not to be used as a synonym of less

letter bomb (hyphenate only in adjectival use)

letterbox, postbox (no hyphens)

leukaemia

Levi's (jeans) should take the apostrophe; but use Levi Strauss for the company

liaison, liaise the word *link* would often be better. The verb *to liaise* has forced its way into the language; however, use sparingly and only in its correct sense – to establish co-operation, to act as a link with, not as a synonym of *meet* or *talk*

Liberal Democrats Lib Dems is an acceptable alternative in either headlines or text. But do not shorten simply to Liberals. Abbreviate in lists etc to LD. *See* Politics special section (page 131)

licence (noun), **license** (verb), but beware of **licensee** (noun), licensed, licensing. *See* practice, practise

Liechtenstein

lifeguard (on a beach); Life Guardsman (on a horse)

lifelong (one word as adjective)

liferaft (one word), as **lifeboat, lifebelt** etc

lifesize(d) (no hyphen)

lift-off (spacecraft etc), as take-off (hyphenated)

light bulb two words as noun, but hyphenate adjectivally

lightning (as in electrical storm), lightening (as in making lighter)

light-year

like do not use as a synonym of *such as* (eg, say "cities such as Manchester are ambitious", not "cities like Manchester ..."); nor as a synonym of *as if* (eg, say "he looks as if he is succeeding", not "he looks like he is succeeding")

likeable

lily of the valley

linchpin (not lynchpin)

liner take care with this word, which strictly no longer applies to passenger cruise ships. Liners nowadays are cargo vessels trading regularly between designated ports, eg, container ships. Confine use of "liner" for passenger ships to historical contexts, eg, the transatlantic liner *Queen Mary*

line-up (noun), but to line up (verb)

Lipizzaner horses (prefer this version to Lippizaner)

liquefy (not liquify), but **liquidate**

liquorice, not the American licorice

lira (singular), **lire** (plural), the former Italian currency

literally avoid as expression of emphasis; "he literally exploded with anger" is absurd

livery halls (in the City of London) do not take the definite article (eg, Drapers' Hall, not the Drapers' Hall). *See* London

living room (no hyphen, as dining room etc)

Livingstone, Ken, Dr (David) Livingstone (explorer), but **Livingston**, West Lothian

Livorno rather than Leghorn, despite usual style on Anglicising foreign names

Llewelyn-Bowen, Laurence, interior designer

Lloyd's of London now use this full name at first mention, Lloyd's thereafter. Note **Lloyd's names**

Lloyds TSB, the bank, but **Lloyd's of London** (insurance)

Lloyd Webber all family members (father William and sons Andrew and Julian) have no hyphen except in reference to Andrew as **Lord Lloyd-Webber**

loan is a noun (ie, never say "I loaned him £20" etc); the verb is lend/lent

loathe (verb), **loath** (adjective; not *loth*)

local government cap councils when full title, eg, Watford Borough Council, Newtown District Council (thereafter the council); but l/c when title is not in full, eg, Watford council; all council committees in l/c; although we cap Mayor at first mention (eg, Albert Hobart, Mayor of Rochdale), l/c for council officials such as borough surveyor, town clerk; cap the seat of local government if we are sure of its title (eg, Leeds City Hall, Birmingham Council House – not to be confused with Birmingham Town Hall – Lambeth Town Hall etc)

lochs in Scotland, but **loughs** in Ireland

Lockerbie suspects the convicted man is Abdul Baset Ali al-Megrahi (after first mention, al-Megrahi); his co-accused was Al-Amin Khalifa Fhimah (thereafter Mr Fhimah)

lockout (in industrial disputes etc), one word; but *to lock out*

locomotive names are italicised, as with ships' or aircraft names, eg, *Mallard*. Do not use "the" unless certain it is part of the name. *See* aircraft names, ships

London   cap the **East End** and the **West End** of London, and now also **North London**, **South London**, **East London**, **West London**, **Central London**, **Inner London**; but l/c southeast London, southwest London etc. The local council for the City of London is the Court of Common Council, whose members are common councilmen; cap Borough in titles of particular boroughs, eg, London Borough of Bromley. *See* livery halls

London Assembly. *See* Greater London Authority

London Clinic, The (cap "T")

London clubs   important to get the names correct as our readership remains strong in clubland. Note particularly **the Athenaeum**; **Boodle's**; **Brooks's**; **Buck's Club**; **Pratt's Club**; **the Queen's Club**; **Royal Over-Seas League**; **Savile Club**; **Travellers Club**; **United Oxford and Cambridge University Club**; **White's Club**. It would be wrong to say, eg, Boodle's Club; on the other hand, it is permissible to refer to the Garrick Club, the Reform Club, the Savage Club etc simply as the Garrick, the Reform or the Savage

Londonderry. *See* Ireland

London hotels and **restaurants** as with London clubs, it is essential to give the correct form of the following: **Berkeley Hotel**; **Brown's Hotel**; **Claridge's**; **the Dorchester**; **Four Seasons Hotel**; **Le Meridien Grosvenor House**; **Hilton London Kensington** (one of some 16 Hiltons in the capital); **Hyatt Carlton Tower hotel**; **Mandarin Oriental Hyde Park Hotel**; **The Lanesborough**; **Langham Hilton**; **Le Meridien Piccadilly**; **London Hilton on Park Lane**; **Marriott Hotel** (several in the capital); **May Fair Inter-Continental Hotel**; **New**

Connaught Rooms; **Sheraton Park Lane Hotel**; **Quaglino's**; **Ritz Hotel**; **The Savoy**; **Simpson's-in-the-Strand**; **Le Meridien Waldorf**; **Royal Westmoreland Hotel**

London Stock Exchange may be abbreviated to LSE, but use sparingly and only in context, especially in headlines, because of confusion with the London School of Economics. Prefer the Exchange (initial cap) wherever possible. *See* LSE

London Transport has been rebranded as Transport for London (abbreviate TfL), not Transport in London. *See* Transport

London University the constituent colleges are: Birkbeck College; Courtauld Institute of Art; Goldsmiths College (no apostrophe); Heythrop College; Imperial College of Science, Technology and Medicine (Imperial College, London acceptable shortened form); Institute of Education; King's College London (no comma); London Business School; London School of Economics and Political Science (London School of Economics or LSE acceptable shortened forms); London School of Hygiene and Tropical Medicine; Queen Mary (NB, no College attached); Royal Academy of Music; Royal Holloway (NB, no College attached); Royal Veterinary College; St George's Hospital Medical School; School of Oriental and African Studies; School of Pharmacy; University College London (no comma)

London Zoo (cap Zoo)

Longchamp (not Longchamps), the French racecourse

longstanding do not use hyphen

lookout (noun, no hyphen)

Lord Advocate do not add *for Scotland*

Lord Chancellor's Department (caps, and not Lord Chancellor's Office)

Lord Mayor (caps) as in Lord Mayor of London, Birmingham etc; thereafter, the lord mayor; the same applies to Mayor of Guildford etc

Lord of the Rings, The, by J.R.R. Tolkien. Note *The* is part of the title. *See* Middle-earth, Tolkien

Lord's (cricket ground)

lords justices (both words take the plural)

lord-lieutenant should be hyphenated, according to the Association of Lord-Lieutenants (note this plural, *not* lords-lieutenant); use l/c in general use, but the Lord-Lieutenant of Gloucestershire etc (when specific)

lorry prefer lorry to truck, but the American **truck** has become ubiquitous and cannot be banned, especially from foreign stories

loss-maker, loss-making

Lotto the renamed national lottery. *See* National Lottery, rollover

loveable takes the midde "e", as likeable

Lovells City solicitors, no longer Lovell White Durrant

lowbrow (as highbrow)

Lower House, Upper House (of Parliament). *See* Politics special section (page 131)

low-key

Loya Jirga (roman, initial caps), the Afghan national council that meets irregularly. *See* War on Terror

loyalist. *See* Ireland

LSE short for London School of Economics, or – sparingly and only in context in Business pages – London Stock Exchange. *See* London University

Ltd can usually be dropped from company names (as can plc)

lullaby (not -bye)

lumbar, as in the lower back (eg, lumbar puncture); **lumber** as in junk furniture, lumberjacks, or (verbally) moving clumsily about etc

Lurex (initial cap)

Luton airport (l/c airport), and resist pressure to insert *international*. *See* airports

Luxembourg (not -burg); the inhabitants should be called Mr, Mrs etc, rather than M or Mme (*see* foreign appellations, Santer); but note **Rosa Luxemburg** (leader of Berlin uprising in 1919)

Lycra (cap, proprietary)

lying in state (noun, no hyphens; nor the verb, to lie in state)

Lyons (not Lyon). *See* Marseilles, foreign places

Lyric Theatre Hammersmith (no comma)

-lyse the style is analyse, paralyse etc (not -ize). *See* -ise, -isation

Lytham St Anne's, Lancashire (use the apostrophe, but no hyphens)

Lyttelton Theatre (at the National); similarly, **Humphrey Lyttelton** (jazz musician)

M

M1 do not say M1 motorway

Maastricht treaty (l/c treaty), but Treaty of Maastricht; for an unofficial name for the updated version of the treaty, write Maastricht II (not 2 or Two)

Macau (not Macao)

Macaulay, Sarah (Gordon Brown's wife)

Mac, Mc always check spelling of these prefixes in *Who's Who*; in alphabetical lists, treat Mc as Mac

McCarthy, Senator Joseph; McCarthyism

McCartney, (Sir) Paul

MacDonald, Ramsay

McDonald, (Sir) Trevor, the newsreader

McDonald's, the hamburger chain

McDonnell Douglas (no hyphen)

MacDowell, Andie

Macedonia the correct (and politically sensitive) title of the new republic is the Former Yugoslav Republic of Macedonia (caps as shown). Accept no variations. *See* Yugoslav

Machiavelli(an)

machinegun, but sub-machinegun

MacKay, Andrew, Tory politician (not Mackay)

mackintosh (raincoat)

Mackintosh, (Sir) Cameron

MacLaine, Shirley

Maclean, Donald

McLuhan, Marshall

Macmillan, Harold, and the publishers

Macpherson, Elle

macroeconomic, microeconomic (no hyphen)

Macy's (New York store)

Madame Tussaud's

"mad cow" disease. *See* BSE, Creutzfeldt-Jakob

Madejski Stadium, Reading (not Madjeski)

Madison Square Garden, New York (not Gardens)

Madonna her maiden name is Ciccone (not Ciccione)

maestros (plural of maestro; not maestri)

Mafia cap only in Italian or US

context; l/c mafia in countries such as Russia when used as a synonym of gangsters

Mafikeng the new name (since 1980) of Mafeking. Spell according to historical context

Magdalen College, **Oxford**; but **Magdalene** College, **Cambridge**. *See* Oxford, Cambridge

Maghreb. *See* Middle East

"magic circle", l/c and quotes first mention, for top law firms in the City; but cap **Magic Circle** for the magicians' organisation

magistrates' courts the Metropolitan Magistrate, West London Magistrate etc, but usually magistrates take l/c. An acceptable alternative for a non-stipendiary (ie, lay) magistrate is JP (Justice of the Peace). When the accused is appearing before the bench, he appears before the magistrates (plural) unless a stipendiary magistrate, now called a district judge (magistrates' courts). The full name of the court is capped, as in Bow Street Magistrates' Court. *See* courts, legal terms, Courts special section (page 47)

Magna Carta, not *the* Magna Carta

mailshot

major do not use as a lazy alternative for *big, chief, important* or *main*

Majorca, **Minorca** use the Anglicised forms. *See* Spanish regions

majority of do not use as alternative for *most of*

makeover one word as noun; but try to avoid this cliché – say *remodelling* instead

make-up (cosmetics or typography), not makeup

Malaysia Datuk Seri Dr Mahathir Mohamad, the Prime Minister; thereafter Dr Mahathir

Mall, The (cap "T")

Mammon (initial cap)

Man cap in the context of humankind. *See* Nature

management buyout spell out first time, though MBO (plural MBOs) is acceptable on Business pages

manifestos (not -oes)

Manila, capital of the Philippines

manoeuvre, **manoeuvring**, **manoeuvrable**

mantelpiece (not mantlepiece)

manuscript(s) write out when part of a sentence, but abbreviate to MSS when quotation from catalogue, or in headline if context is clear

Mao Zedong (no longer Mao Tsetung). *See* Chinese names

marathon avoid in clichéd sense of *a long time* as in "a marathon session". Cap as in London Marathon, New York Marathon

march past (noun; two words in military context)

Mardi Gras for the Shrove Tuesday festival, but note the self-styled **Mardi Gra bomber**

Margrethe, Queen of Denmark (not *Margarethe*)

Marines cap in both Royal Marines and US Marines; also, a Marine

marketplace (one word), but market-maker

Marks & Spencer use the ampersand rather than *and* in text; can abbreviate to M&S in headlines; the formal legal title is Marks and Spencer plc, but we need use this form only rarely

marquess, not marquis, except in foreign titles. *See* Titles special section (page 171)

Marrakesh (not Marrakech)

married couple's allowance

Marriott hotels (not Marriot)

Mars bar(s) (l/c "b")

Marseilles (not Marseille); also call the football club Marseilles (not Olympique de Marseille)

Martini is a trade name, so always cap

Marxist, Marxism derived from Karl Marx, so cap. Do not use as loose variant of communism. *See* communism

Mary Celeste (not *Marie Celeste*)

Mass (cap in its religious context), also Holy Mass, Requiem Mass etc. *See* Churches special section (page 37)

Massachusetts

massive avoid as a synonym of *big*

MasterCard

masterclass (musical etc; no hyphen)

master of foxhounds (l/c). *See* foxhunt

Master of the Queen's Music

Master of the Rolls. *See* Courts special section (page 47)

Matabele singular and plural (a Matabele, the Matabele people)

materialise avoid as a synonym of *appear, come about* or *happen*

Mathews, Meg (ex-wife of Noel Gallagher)

matinee (no accent), as premiere, debut, decor etc. *See* Arts special section (page 18)

matins (l/c). *See* evensong, Christian terms

matt (not mat), as in matt paint, matt black etc

Maupassant, Guy de

Mauretania, the liner; **Mauritania**, the country

may/might do not confuse; use *might* in sentences referring to past possibilities that did not happen, eg, "If that had happened ten days ago, my whole life might have been different". A clear distinction is evident in the following example: "He might have been captured by the Iraqis – but he wasn't", compared with "He may have been captured by the Iraqis – it is possible but we don't know"

Maya, one of the Indian people of Central America; **Mayas**, plural; and **Mayan**, adjective

mayday (as in SOS), l/c; but **May Day** (holiday)

Mayfair, but May Fair Inter-Continental Hotel. *See* London hotels

mayor for when to cap, *see* local government, Lord Mayor. But note that the **Mayor of London** becomes the mayor (l/c) after first mention

Maze prison in Northern Ireland; do not use Long Kesh except in quotes or historical context

MCC, short for Marylebone Cricket Club. Do not say **the** MCC

mealtimes write breakfast time, lunchtime, teatime, dinner time,

supper time (but use hyphens in compounds when adjectival)

means-test, **means-tested** etc (hyphenate whether as noun, verb or adjective)

means to an end is singular; but "his means *are* modest"

Médecins sans Frontières

media, plural as in mass media, but mediums (spiritualists)

medical officer of health MoH acceptable in headlines

medical terms never use these metaphorically or as terms of abuse (geriatric, paralytic, schizophrenic). In words ending in -tomy (appendectomy, hysterectomy etc), the word "operation" is tautologous and must not be used. *See* bacteria, X-ray

medieval (not mediaeval)

Mediterranean

meet never say *meet with*

mega- be very sparing with this as a colloquial prefix meaning *big*

megawatts the capacity of a power station is measured in megawatts; the output is measured in megawatt hours. The correct abbreviation of megawatt is MW (not mW, which means milliwatt). *See* kilowatt-hour

mêlée

Member of Parliament (cap Member), but MP almost always preferable

mementoes (not -os)

memoirs (not memoires)

memorandum, plural memorandums (not -a)

meningitis distinguish whether bacterial or viral; the headline cases are usually bacterial

Mercedes-Benz (hyphen)

Merchant Navy (caps)

Merchant Taylors' School (both Middlesex and Liverpool)

Merthyr Tydfil in South Wales (now a unitary authority) must never be shortened to Merthyr, which is a village in Carmarthenshire. *See* unitary authorities, Wales

Messerschmitt (not -schmidt)

mete out (not meet out), in context of punishment

Method acting use cap "M"

metres, as in distance, poetry etc; **meters**, as in gas, electricity or parking etc

metric *The Times* should keep abreast of the trend in the UK to move gradually towards all-metric use, but given the wide age range of our readers, some continuing use of imperial measurements is still necessary. The main aim is to avoid confusing the reader, so try not to mix the two systems in a single article. In general, we should **prefer the metric, with imperial conversions in brackets at first mention**. This should now apply particularly to **temperatures**, eg, the temperature on the South Coast hit the low 30s [no longer nineties]; but where specific, eg, 16C (61F). Similarly, for **areas** prefer hectares and square metres to acres and square yards, but do not use square kilometres in the UK and the US where distances are measured in miles.

However, the following will remain (for the time being) the **principal exceptions**:

1. **Distances globally**. Give miles first, and convert (at first mention) to kilometres in brackets for all countries apart from the UK and the US. **Speeds**: use only miles per hour (mph) in the UK and US; for all other countries use mph but also convert to kilometres per hour (km/h) in brackets at first mention

2. **Personal measurements in height and weight**. Continue to say she was 5ft 7in (1.7m) and weighed 9st 10lb (62kg)

3. **Altitude and depth**: The main exception to metric should be **aircraft altitude**, where a pilot will announce that "we are now flying at 33,000ft"; metric

conversion to 10,058m may be used in brackets here. But now specify **mountain heights in metric** first, eg, Ben Nevis is the highest peak in Britain at 1,343m (4,406ft)

4. **Volume**: The main exceptions to metric should be **pints of beer and cider**, while milk (confusingly) is still sold in pint bottles as well as litre containers. With **petrol and fuel** now sold in litres rather than gallons, use metric, eg, 75p a litre (no longer any need to convert), but because car manufacturers still do so, give **fuel consumption** in miles per gallon.

From now on, the overwhelming preference is **sporting, foreign, engineering and scientific stories to be metric**; similarly **foodstuffs and liquids in cookery** contexts, recipes etc should be metric, though small amounts can be given in tablespoons (tbsp) and teaspoons (tsp).

The most common metric abbreviations are mm (millimetre), cm (centimetre), m (metre) and km (kilometre); mg (milligram), g (gram), kg (kilogram); sq m (square metre), ha (hectare), sq km (square kilometre), cu m (cubic metre); ml (millilitre), cl (centilitre), l (litre); W (watt), kW (kilowatt). *Never* add a final "s" to any of these abbreviations, eg, 48km (*not* 48kms)

Metropolitan Police (*see*

Commissioner); Metropolitan Magistrate (*see* magistrates' courts)

Michelangelo

microchip

microgram do not abbreviate, and certainly not to mcg, which is meaningless under international scientific standard abbreviations

microlight (prefer to microlite)

mid-air (hyphenate, noun or adjective)

midday, midweek (no hyphens)

Middle Ages, the (caps)

Middle-earth. *See Lord of the Rings*, Tolkien

Middle East comprises Bahrain, Cyprus, Egypt, Iran, Iraq, Israel, Jordan, Kuwait, Lebanon, Oman, Qatar, Saudi Arabia, Sudan, Syria, Turkey, United Arab Emirates, Yemen. In a general sense, it also takes in the countries of the Maghreb: Algeria, Libya, Mauritania, Morocco, Tunisia, Western Sahara. Never abbreviate to the Americanism *Mideast*

Middle England (caps, in political context)

Middlesbrough

Middlesex is no longer a county. *See* postal addresses

Mideast unacceptable as abbreviation of Middle East

Mid Glamorgan (no hyphen) no longer exists as a local government authority, but name persists in some organisations and titles, eg, Lord-Lieutenant of Mid Glamorgan. *See* unitary authorities

Midland Bank no longer exists as a trading entity. It is part of HSBC, so use Midland only in historical context. *See* Hong Kong

midlife crisis but do not overuse this cliché

midnight (not 12 midnight). *See* noon

midsummer, **midwinter**

Midwest (US)

MiG, the former Soviet aircraft

migrant do not use in place of *emigrant* or *immigrant*. It means one who is in the process of migrating

mike (not mic), as abbreviation for microphone

mileage

military ranks use hyphens in compounds such as Major-General, Lieutenant-Colonel etc (where two ranks are joined), but not with Second Lieutenant, Lance Corporal, Air Commodore etc. Do not abbreviate ranks except in lists. Refer, eg, to Major-General Geoffrey Blimp, Lieutenant-Colonel Godfrey Blank at first mention, thereafter General Blimp, Colonel

Blank; similarly, Rear-Admiral Horatio Salt, thereafter Admiral Salt. *See* Armed Forces special section (page 14)

militate (against or in favour of); do not confuse with mitigate

millennium common usage says that the millennium ended on December 31, 1999, though technically it should have been December 31, 2000. We should accept the former. Note the Millennium Dome (and Dome at all other times too), Millennium Fund, Millennium Commission, Millennium Exhibition (caps). Also Millennium Eve (as New Year's Eve). Also Millennium Wheel (as with the Dome), even though its official name is the London Eye. Note also the Millennium Bridge over the Thames. The plural of millennium is **millennia** (unlike memorandums etc; *see* referendum). Note also **millenarian** (only one middle "n") meaning of, or related to, the millennium. *See* zones

millions write out millions from one to ten, thereafter 11 million etc. Abbreviate to "m" only for headlines. For currencies, spell out in text, eg, £15 million, but abbreviate to £15m in headlines. With decimal notations, best to restrict to two decimal points in text, rounded up or down (eg, £1.53 million), though in headlines try to avoid decimals altogether. In text, write 2.5 million rather than spelling out two and a half million; but "three million shares changed hands" (not 3 million shares) etc

Mind, the mental health charity (no longer MIND). But *see* SANE, initials

mindset is a cliché; prefer *mentality*

minimal do not use as a synonym of *small*; it means smallest, or the least possible in size, duration etc

miniskirt (no hyphen); also, **minicab**

ministers (political) cap all ministers, whether in the Cabinet or not. The same applies to ministers in overseas governments: give name and full title (capped) first time, thereafter name or just "the minister". *See* Politics special section (page 131)

Minnelli, Liza

minuscule (not miniscule). Originally, a medieval script. Use sparingly, as it is heavily overworked as a synonym of *very small* or *unimportant*

Mishcon de Reya, solicitors (l/c "de")

mis-hit (hyphen), **mis-sell**; but *see* misspell

Miss, Ms Ms is nowadays fully acceptable when a woman (married or unmarried) wants to be called

thus, or when it is not known for certain if she is Mrs or Miss. Ms is increasingly common in American and UK contexts. *See* appellations

missiles Pakistan's missiles are the Hatf (short-range), Shaheen (short), Ghaznavi (medium) and Ghauri (medium). India's are the Prithvi (short-range) and Agni (medium). Most of the above may have numerals after them, eg, Shaheen2

Mississippi

misspell (no hyphen); *see* spelt

mitigate means to *make milder*, *moderating* (as in mitigating circumstances in a law case); not to be confused with militate

Mitterrand, François, the late French President

moccasins (not mocassins)

MoD acceptable abbreviation for Ministry of Defence, especially in headlines

Moët & Chandon (no longer Moët et Chandon)

Mogul (not Mughal) for the empire and art

Mohammed. *See* Muhammad

Moldova (no longer Moldavia)

Mona Lisa (not Monna Lisa)

monarch (l/c) for the British monarch; but the Sovereign, the Crown. *See* Royal Family

Mönchengladbach (no hyphen), rather than the former spelling of München-Gladbach

Monetary Policy Committee (caps) of the Bank of England; MPC at subsequent mentions

moneys (plural of money), but money will usually serve. Also, **moneyed**, not monied

money-laundering

Mongol, **Mongolian**, for the race. Never refer to a Down's syndrome sufferer as a mongol

Monopolies and Mergers Commission (MMC) is now renamed the **Competition Commission**. Refer to the MMC now only in historical context

Monsignor (Mgr abbreviated) can now be used for Roman Catholic archbishops or bishops in Britain (where appropriate), as well as in foreign contexts. *See* Churches special section (page 37)

Montagu of Beaulieu, Lord

Montenegrin is the adjective from Montenegro (not Montenegran)

months abbreviate (only in lists or listings) as follows: Jan, Feb, March, April, May, June, July, Aug, Sept, Oct, Nov, Dec

Moon cap in planetary context, otherwise l/c. *See* Earth, Sun, Universe

Moral Re-Armament (not Rearmament), MRA at subsequent mentions

more than always use rather than *over* with numbers, eg, "more than 2,500 people attended the rally", not "over 2,500 …"

Moreton-in-Marsh (not Morton, nor -in-the-)

MORI must cap

Morissette, Alanis

Morrell, Lady Ottoline (not Otteline)

morris dancing/dancers

Morse code

mortar do not use by itself when the meaning is mortar bomb; the mortar is the launcher from which the shell is fired. But mortar attack is perfectly correct

mosquitoes (not -os as plural)

most favoured nation status

MoT certificate, test; but the Department for Transport, or Transport Department (not Ministry of …)

Mother Nature (initial caps). *See* Nature

Mother Teresa (*not* Theresa)

Mother's Day, or Mothering Sunday (not Mothers')

motocross (not motorcross)

motorcycle, motorcyclist, motorbike etc

motoring terms the following terms should be standardised throughout the paper thus: **carburettor, wheelspin, four-wheel drive** (shorten to **4WD**), but a **four-wheel-drive vehicle** (two hyphens when adjectival), **power steering, anti-lock brakes, 3-litre car, 1.9 diesel** (hyphenated when adjectival), **four-door, hatchback, four-star petrol, E-type Jaguar, Mercedes-Benz E-class** etc, **airbag, seatbelt, numberplate, sports car**.
For the foreseeable future, continue to give fuel consumption figures in miles per gallon. *See* metric

motor neurone disease (not neuron)

moveable (keep middle "e")

movies, although an Americanism, is now so common as to be an acceptable synonym of *films*; but use *films* whenever possible

, MP, QC, commas each side when used after name. Plural MPs (never MP's). *See* Member of Parliament, Politics special section (page 131), Courts special section (page 47)

Mr, Mrs, Miss, Ms. *See* appellations

mugging strictly means theft by violence in the open air. Take care not to overuse

Muhammad use this spelling for the Prophet, but respect the other spellings of the name according to individuals' preference; if in doubt, use Muhammad. Note also **Muhammad Ali** but **King Mohammed VI of Morocco**. *See* names

Muhammad al-Masari (Saudi dissident); then Dr Masari

Mullah Muhammad Omar supreme leader of the Taleban; Mullah Omar at subsequent mention. *See* War on Terror

Mujahidin (cap), the fighters in a jihad or holy war

multi incline towards making *multi* compounds one word wherever possible, whether used as a noun or as an adjective, eg, multimillionaire, multinational, multilateral, multimedia, multiracial, multispeed, multistorey, multitrack (and note **multispeed, multitrack Europe**). However, when the compound appears too hideous, such as multi-ethnic, hyphenate. **Multimillion-pound** (multimillion-dollar) deal etc

mum. *See* dad and mum

Murdoch, Elisabeth refer to her as Ms Murdoch at subsequent mentions

Murdoch, Rupert at first mention he should be described as chairman and chief executive of The News Corporation, parent company of *The*

Times. See News International, *The Times*

Murphy-O'Connor, Cardinal Cormac, Archbishop of Westminster. Note hyphen

Musharraf, General Pervez (not Pervaiz), President of Pakistan from 2001. Refer to him as General Musharraf after first mention

musical vocabulary

a. song titles (classical or pop), album titles, operas (including arias), take italics

b. symphonies Symphony No 3 (roman, caps); but where symphonies have numbers and

popular alternative titles (Eroica, Pastoral) the titles, when used, are in italics, eg, *Eroica*

c. concertos First Violin Concerto (roman caps). For fuller list, *see* Arts special section (page 18)

music-hall

Muslim, not Moslem or Mohamedan. *See* Islam, Muhammad

Mussorgsky, Modest (prefer to Moussorgsky)

Muzak (cap, proprietary)

Myanmar continue to call the country Burma

mynah bird (prefer to mina, myna)

N

Naafi the Navy, Army and Air Force Institutes; commonly used as the canteen for Service personnel run by the Naafi

Nafta North American Free Trade Agreement (not Area or Association)

naive, naivety (no diaeresis)

names as a general rule, people are entitled to be known as they wish to be known, provided their identities are clear. Thus Cassius Clay became Muhammad Ali; but in such changes, give both names until the new one is widely known. Note Lloyd's names (l/c). *See* appellations, Lloyd's

names starting stories cap both names, as GORDON BROWN said last night ... (not GORDON Brown said ...). Where the name is too long to contain in the first line, reconstruct the sentence to place the name away from the start

narcotics take care to use this word correctly. *See* drugs

Nasa National Aeronautics and Space Administration (US); rarely necessary to spell out nowadays

national avoid as a synonym of *citizen*, as in a French national

National Air Traffic Services (caps and note plural), or the air traffic control service (informal alternative, l/c). Abbreviate to Nats, rather than NATS

National Anthem now initial caps for the UK anthem, *God Save the Queen*

National Association of Schoolmasters and Union of Women Teachers (full title), then NASUWT (no slash)

national curriculum (l/c)

National Health Service, the NHS, or the health service (NHS for headlines)

national insurance (l/c, like other taxes), in general context, but caps for National Insurance Fund

National Lottery has changed its name (May 2002) to Lotto. Use the phrase National Lottery now only in historical context, or l/c national lottery as a generic phrase (eg, Lotto, the national lottery). Note also the National Lottery Charities Board is now known as the Community Fund. *See* Lotto, rollover

national missile defence (NMD), the US missile defence project (l/c when spelt out)

National Parks should be capped only with specific names (eg,

Snowdonia National Park; but "the policy applies particularly to national parks")

National Rivers Authority (not River)

National Savings & Investments (NS&I), the savings organisation (no longer simply National Savings)

National Security Adviser cap this top post in US political context

National Service (caps)

National Statistics is the new agency (June 2000) incorporating the Office for National Statistics. The boss is called the National Statistician; the agency watchdog is the Statistics Commission. *See* Office for National Statistics

National Theatre (caps); generally omit Royal. *See* Lyttelton

nationalist l/c except when referring to name of a political party. Thus Scottish National Party (SNP) and Scottish Nationalists. But in Irish contexts, l/c. *See* Ireland

nationwide no hyphen, but use sparingly as it borders on being a cliché; prefer national or nationally. *See* wide

Native American cap the "N" when referring to American Indians

Nato (never NATO)

Nature cap sparingly, only in the context of personifying the power that creates and regulates the world. Also, Mother Nature

NatWest is an acceptable abbreviation for National Westminster Bank in text or headlines

naught, come to (not *nought*, which means the digit 0)

nave is a central space in a church; journalists who misspell the word are knaves

navy, naval the Royal Navy (thereafter the Navy capped); the Merchant Navy, the US Navy, the Brazilian Navy etc (thereafter the navy, l/c, for all of these); *naval* is l/c except in titles such as Royal Naval Volunteer Reserve (RNVR) etc. *See* officers, ships, warships, Armed Forces special section (page 14)

Nazi, Nazism (caps). *See* communist

Neanderthal (cap, and not -tal)

nearby, near by the first is adjectival, eg, "the nearby school was convenient"; the second is adverbial, eg, "he sat on a bench near by"

nearly one in three … is prefer singular to plural *are* in these constructions. *See* one

Needles, The but *see* Solent

Neighbourhood Watch

neither takes a singular verb, eg,

"neither is …", "neither Bert nor Fred has any idea". Do not use the construction neither … or … (must use nor). *See* none

Nepad the New Partnership for Africa's Development (not African)

nerve-racking (not -wracking). *See* racked, wrack

Nestlé

Netanyahu, Binyamin (not Benjamin), Israeli politician

Net Book Agreement (caps)

Netherlands, the (no longer cap The). Do not use Holland as an alternative except in sporting or historical contexts. *See* Holland

Network SouthEast no longer exists

nevertheless (one word, as nonetheless)

new frequently redundant. Try the sentence without it and see if it really adds any meaning; always omit in "setting a *new* record"

New Age travellers (no quotes). *See* Gypsy, travellers

newborn (as in babies, no hyphen)

Newcastle upon Tyne, Newcastle-under-Lyme

New Deal caps for Labour's welfare programme; quotes at first mention if appropriate

newfound (no hyphen)

Newhaven, East Sussex, but New Haven, Connecticut

new Labour l/c "n", quotes not usually necessary, except when the writer or speaker is making a particular, perhaps ironic, point. But keep caps in slogans such as "New Labour, New Danger". *See* Politics special section (page 131)

newscaster prefer newsreader

News International Rupert Murdoch is chairman and chief executive of The News Corporation (second mention, News Corp). News Corp can be described as "parent company of *The Times*". A subsidiary of News Corp is News International, a British company that owns Times Newspapers Holdings. The operating subsidiary of Times Newspapers Holdings is Times Newspapers Ltd, publisher of *The Times* and *The Sunday Times*. Times Newspapers Holdings is chaired by Mr Murdoch (the vice-chairman is Sir Edward Pickering) and the board includes the independent national directors of *The Times* and *The Sunday Times*. It is thus the controlling company.

News Group Newspapers, another operating subsidiary of News International, is the publisher of *The Sun* and *News of the World* (and *Sunday Magazine*).

TSL Education Ltd (formerly Times Supplements Ltd) is another operating subsidiary of News

International and is the publisher of *The Times Educational Supplement*, *The Times Higher Education Supplement*, *The Times Literary Supplement*, *Nursery World*, *TES College Manager* and *TES Primary* magazine. Worldwide Learning Ltd, a subsidiary of TSL Education, is a provider of global distance learning solutions.

News Ltd is the Australian arm of News Corp. Mr Murdoch does not "own" any of these companies, though his family is the largest single (though not majority) shareholder in News Corp. *See* BSkyB, Murdoch, *The Times*

newspapers and journals; use italics for titles and make sure to use The in the title whenever appropriate. The lists that follow, though not exhaustive, should cover the most frequently mentioned:

a. **With The in the masthead**:
The Times, *The Sunday Times*, *The Sun*, *The Guardian*, *The Independent*, *The Independent on Sunday*, *The Daily Telegraph*, *The Sunday Telegraph*, *The Observer*, *The Mail on Sunday*, *The People*, *The European*, *The Scotsman*, *The Herald* (formerly *The Glasgow Herald*), *The Birmingham Post*, *The Journal* (Newcastle), *The Northern Echo*, *The Argus* (Brighton) (no longer *Evening Argus*), *The Irish Times*, *The Spectator*, *The Economist*, *The Lancet*, *The Sporting Life*, *The Big Issue*

b. **Without The in the masthead**: *News of the World*,

Financial Times, *Daily Mirror* (no longer *The Mirror*, spring 2002), *Daily Mail*, *Daily Express* (May 2000), *Daily Star*, *Daily Sport*, *Sunday Sport*, *Sunday Mirror*, *Sunday Express*, *Evening Standard*, *Scotland on Sunday*, *Yorkshire Post*, *Daily Post* (Liverpool), *Manchester Evening News*, *Western Daily Press* (Bristol), *Western Mail* (Cardiff), *Western Morning News* (Plymouth), *Evening Mail* (Birmingham), *Express & Star* (Wolverhampton), *Telegraph & Argus* (Bradford), *Oxford Mail*, *Sunday Herald* (Glasgow), *Sunday Independent* (Dublin), *New Statesman & Society* (although just *New Statesman* is usually acceptable), *British Medical Journal* (the *BMJ*), *Jewish Chronicle*, *Which?*, *Which Car?* etc, *Racing Post*

c. **Abroad**
The Boston Globe
Chicago Tribune
Los Angeles Times
The Miami Herald
The New York Times
Daily News (New York)
New York Post
The New Yorker
The Washington Post
USA Today
The Wall Street Journal
International Herald Tribune
The Globe and Mail (Toronto)
Bild am Sonntag
Stern
Der Spiegel
Die Welt
Svenska Dagbladet

Izvestia
The Times of India
El País
Le Monde
Le Figaro
L'Espresso (Italy)
Corriere della Sera
Far Eastern Economic Review (Hong Kong)
South China Morning Post (Hong Kong)
The Straits Times (Singapore)
New Straits Times (Malaysia)
The Australian (Sydney)
The Sydney Morning Herald
The Age (Melbourne)
Herald Sun (Melbourne)
The Jerusalem Post
Al-Ahram (Cairo)

d. When the journal's name is used adjectivally, omit The, eg, the *Times* reporter was attacked …

e. Always properly attribute material from another newspaper: never say "a report in another newspaper …" but "a report in *The Guardian* …" etc. However, the general phrases *media reports* or *press reports* are acceptable when material has been widely disseminated

New Year Honours or **New Year's Honours List** (caps); also **the Queen's Birthday Honours** (caps). *See* honours

New Year's Day, **New Year's Eve**, but the **new year** and **Chinese new year**

New York City, **New York State**

(caps), to distinguish them; usually New York will be sufficient for the city, and upstate New York is permissible. Normally, l/c state in contexts such as the state of Virginia, but *see* Washington

New Zealand never NZ, even in headlines

NHS Plan the Government's new health policy (2000). Italicise only with reference to the document itself, *The NHS Plan*

NICE, the National Institute for Clinical Excellence

Nicolson, Sir Harold; but **Jack Nicholson**, the actor

Nietzsche

nightclub

nightmare use only in its proper sense of an unpleasant dream, not as a lazy cliché for something that goes wrong

night-time (hyphen), but **daytime** (one word)

Nikkei average

Nimby(ism) acronym for "not in my backyard", initial cap

Nissan cars, but **Nissen hut**

No 10, or **10 Downing Street** not Number 10 or Downing St. *See* Downing Street, Politics special section (page 131)

"no" campaign (note quotes and l/c), the anti-euro lobby group that also believes the UK should remain in the EU

no-fly zone

no man's land

no-no

no one (two words, no hyphen)

"no" vote, "yes" vote

"no win, no fee" legislation/ agreement etc. *See* Courts special section (page 47)

Nobel Prize for Literature, Medicine etc; or Nobel Peace/ Literature Prize, but Nobel prize (unspecific), Nobel prizewinner, Nobel laureate (l/c "l"), Nobel prize-winning author etc

nonagenarian (not nono-)

noncommittal (no hyphen)

nonconformist, but the Nonconformist Church and Nonconformist churches (buildings). *See* Churches special section (page 37)

non-cooperation. *See* co-operate

none almost always takes the singular verb, eg, "none is available at present". However, very occasionally a plural is permissible, eg, "None of them are better singers than the Welsh" or "none of them have done their best" (where the inelegant alternative would be "none of them has done his or her best"). *See* neither

nonetheless (one word)

non-existent

non-profitmaking

non-stop (hyphenate)

noon (not 12 noon); and never say 12am or 12pm. *See* midnight

normalcy avoid; say normality instead

north, northeast, northern etc; for when to cap, *see* compass points

northerner, southerner (l/c)

Northern Ireland. *See* Ireland

Northumberland, the county; Northumbria is a health, police or tourist authority

North West Frontier Province, in Pakistan (NWFP acceptable after first mention); note initial caps, no hyphens

North York Moors (not North Yorkshire Moors). *See* Yorkshire

notable (no middle "e")

Note cap in the diplomatic sense

not only ... to be followed by **but** (and usually) **also**; often better to say simply **both ... and**

nought. *See* naught

nuclear terms should be used with precision. Take special care not to confuse **fission** and **fusion**

numbers write from one to ten in full, 11 upwards as numerals except when they are approximations, eg, "about thirty people turned up". Keep consistency within a sentence: say "the number injured rose from eight to fourteen", and do not mix fractions and decimals. At the start of a sentence, write all numbers in full; **ordinals**: write out up to twentieth, then 21st, 33rd, 95th etc. But birthdays and anniversaries, write out up to tenth, then 11th, 45th etc. Note 42nd Street, 38th parallel etc.

See birthday, millions, currencies, fractions

numberplate (on vehicles etc; one word). *See* motoring terms

Nuremberg (not -burg)

Nursing, Royal College of (not Nurses)

NVQ national vocational qualification (l/c when spelt out)

O

oast house (two words)

Oath of Allegiance as sworn by new MPs; the oath at subsequent mentions

oblivious of (not "to"); means forgetful of, unaware of. It does not mean ignorant or uncomprehending

O'Brien, Conor Cruise; likewise **Edna**

obscenities "four-letter words" and profanities should be avoided because they upset many readers. However, in direct quotes and where they are essential to the story, style obscenities thus with asterisks: f★★★, f★★★ing, c★★★ etc

occupied territories, the (all l/c)

occurred (not occured)

o'clock. *See* times

octogenarian

octopuses (plural of octopus, not octopi)

Oder-Neisse Line (the boundary between Poland and Germany)

Odone, Cristina (not Christina), journalist

OECD, the Organisation for Economic Co-operation and Development

Oeic (open-ended investment company), cap as with Tessas and Isas

of avoid expressions such as "all of the people attending", "half of the children replied"; say simply "all the people", "half the children" etc

of all time do not use this meaningless phrase, as in "best golfer of all time", in any circumstances

offbeat (no hyphen)

Office for National Statistics formerly the Central Statistical Office, is now part of the agency called National Statistics. *See* National Statistics

Office for Standards in Education, but Ofsted usually sufficient on its own. *See* regulators

officers (naval and military) do not call ratings or NCOs *officers*, especially in headlines and captions. *See* Armed Forces special section (page 14)

oil-drilling, **oil-fired**, **oil-slick**, **oil-tanker**, but **oildrum**, **oilfield**, **oilrig**, **oil platform**. *See* Brent Spar

oil-seed rape (use hyphen)

OK rather than *okay*

old. *See* elderly

Old Etonian, **Old Harrovian** etc

Old Masters (caps to avoid confusion)

Olivier, Laurence (not Lawrence), the late Lord Olivier

Olympics can be used as a short form of the Olympic Games. Similarly, the **Games** (always capped) can be used (same rule for Games in Commonwealth Games etc). Always cap Olympics and Olympic even when used adjectivally, eg, an Olympic athlete. Note International Olympic Committee (no final "s" on Olympic)

ombudsman, **ombudswoman** keep l/c in general context, eg, "he referred the matter to the ombudsman"; but cap for specifics, as in the Local Government Ombudsman, the Legal Services Ombudsman, and even the unofficial title of Parliamentary Ombudsman (the Parliamentary Commissioner for Administration). Do not confuse the Parliamentary Ombudsman with the Parliamentary Commissioner for Standards, an entirely separate post. Note that the **Financial Ombudsman Service** has replaced the Banking, Building Societies, Insurance, Investment, Pensions, and PIA Ombudsmen

on behalf of is a frequently misused phrase. It means *in the interest of* (a person etc) or *as representative of* (eg, "acting on behalf of his client" is correct). It must not be used as a verbose way of saying *by*; eg, "the book betrays a lack of understanding on behalf of the author" is wrong

ONdigital no longer exists

one use the singular verb in structures such as "one in three says that …". *See* nearly. In first-person pieces, try to avoid the use of *one* as a synonym of *I*

one member, one vote (no hyphens). *See* Politics special section (page 131)

One Nation Tories, **One Nation politicians** etc (cap O and N)

one-time do not use as synonym of *former* as in "one-time chairman" etc

One 2 One, the former mobile phone company (note spaces)

ongoing avoid this ugly adjective; say *continuing* if anything is necessary

online one word in computer context

only take great care to place only before the word or phrase it qualifies; "she **only** touched the key, but did not press it; she touched **only** the key, not the switch; she touched the **only** key". Similarly, "he only played cricket" is wrong; "he played only cricket" is correct

on to unlike *into*, two words invariably better than one, as in "she moved on to better things", though "he collapsed onto the floor" is just acceptable. As a general rule, try to stem the advance of **onto**

Opec, the Organisation of Petroleum Exporting Countries

opencast mining

open-heart surgery; **open-door** policy (if this overworked phrase has to be used); **open-plan** living room

"open skies" (l/c, quotes at first mention only), international airline bilateral access agreements

operations. *See* medical terms

ophthalmologist, ophthalmic etc (not opthalmic)

Opposition the same cap or l/c rules apply as to Government – cap as a noun but generally l/c as adjective; eg, "He accused the Opposition of lying", but "He said it was an opposition lie". *See* Politics special section (page 131)

or need not be preceded by *either*, though it is strengthened thereby if two options are mentioned. Usually avoid a comma before it

oral must not be confused with **verbal**; it means pertaining to the mouth, often in the spoken context (eg, the oral tradition, by word of mouth); verbal means pertaining to words (contrasted with, eg, physical or choral). Take care. *See* verbal

Orders in Council are approved, not signed, by the Queen

organic food never say that organic farmers use no chemicals; they frequently use a limited range

ordinals. *See* numbers

Ordnance Survey, and ordnance in military contexts; but **ordinance** as in regulations

Orient, the wherever possible, say the East. The adjective is **oriental**, l/c. The East London football club is Leyton Orient

orientate, orientation prefer this to *orient, oriented* etc. *See* disorientate

Orkney or the Orkney Islands, not the Orkneys. *See* Shetland

Oscar Award(s), or **the Oscars**, caps, as they are registered trademarks. *See* arts awards

OSCE, the Organisation for Security and Co-operation in Europe, has replaced the former CSCE (Conference on Security and Co-operation in Europe)

Ouija (board) takes the cap as it is proprietary

Outback, the (in Australia)

outdoor (adjective); but the outdoors

outpatients, inpatients (no hyphen)

OutRage!, the homosexual "outing" group

outside *never say* outside of

-out suffixes in nouns, generally join up rather than hyphenate, as in **fallout, knockout, printout, callout, dropout, bailout** etc (but to fall out etc)

Outward Bound must be used *only* when referring specifically to the work or courses of the Outward Bound Trust Ltd, and never in general use in phrases such as *outward bound-style activities*. Use alternatives such as *outdoor pursuits, adventure training, outdoor adventure courses* etc. Outward Bound's lawyers pounce on every perceived infringement of its service mark. Take care

over do not use as a synonym of *more than* when followed by a number, eg, "she waited over four hours for the train" should be "… more than four hours …"; "there were over 60 victims" should be "… more than 60 …". *See* more than

over as prefix wherever the word does not look too ugly, dispense with the hyphen, even when this leads to a double "r" in the middle; thus, **overcapacity, overestimate, overreact, override, overrule, overuse, overvalue**; an obvious exception where the hyphen is essential is **over-age**

overall one word as adjective, but use sparingly

overly do not use as an alternative for *over* or *too*

Overseas Development Administration (not Agency) no longer exists; it has been subsumed into the Department for International Development. *See* departments

owing to. *See* due to

Oxbridge be sparing in using the term as a "catch-all" for Oxford and Cambridge Universities

Oxford University colleges and halls are:
All Souls College; Balliol College; Blackfriars; Brasenose College; Campion Hall; Christ Church; Corpus Christi College; Exeter College; Green College; Greyfriars; Harris Manchester College; Hertford College; Jesus College; Keble College; Kellogg College; Lady Margaret Hall; Linacre College; Lincoln College; Magdalen College; Mansfield College; Merton College; New College; Nuffield College; Oriel College; Pembroke College; The Queen's College; Regent's Park College; St Anne's College; St Antony's College; St Benet's Hall; St Catherine's College; St Cross College; St Edmund Hall; St Hilda's College; St Hugh's College; St John's College; St Peter's College; Somerville College; Templeton College; Trinity College; University College; Wadham College; Wolfson College; Worcester College; Wycliffe Hall

P

p's and q's. *See* apostrophes

Pacific Rim, **South Pacific**, **North Pacific** etc

paedophile, an adult sexually attracted to children, but **pederast**, a man who has sexual relations with boys. Do not confuse

page 1, **page 3**, **page 187** etc, but a **Page 3 Girl**

Page, Jennie (not Jenny)

paintings titles in italic. *See* Arts special section (page 18)

Pakistani can be used both for the people of Pakistan and adjectivally, eg, Pakistani culture

palace cap in full names, such as Blenheim Palace, thereafter the palace – except that the Palace is to be used for Buckingham Palace in stories about royalty. *See* Royal Family

Palace of Holyroodhouse, Edinburgh

palaeo- (not paleo-), so palaeography etc

palaeontology concerns the study of fossils and must not be confused with archaeology, which concerns human cultural remains

Palestinian National Authority (not Palestine) – usually the Palestinian Authority will suffice; but the **Palestine Liberation Organisation** (the PLO)

Palme d'Or, top prize at the Cannes Film Festival

Palmer-Tomkinson, Tara

palmtop (computers etc)

pantyhose, but normally write tights

paparazzi

paperboy, **papergirl**

paraffin. *See* kerosene

paraphernalia (not *paraphanalia*)

paratroops a general term for troops dropped by parachute; a parachutist is a specialist in the activity. Note, The Parachute Regiment

Pardo Palace is a royal palace on the outskirts of Madrid; the Madrid art gallery is the **Prado**

Parent's Charter

Paris some of the more familiar place names prone to error are the **Champs Elysées**, the **Elysée Palace**, the **Quai d'Orsay**, the **Jardin du Luxembourg** (not de), the **Jardin des Tuileries** (not de)

and the **Jeu de Paume** (not Pomme)

Parker Bowles, Camilla (no hyphen)

Parkinson's disease

Parliament cap always in British context, and in overseas contexts when the word forms part of the institution, eg, the European Parliament, Canadian Parliament. However, l/c in such as the Spanish parliament (the Cortes), the Russian parliament (Duma), the Israeli parliament (Knesset), Polish parliament (Sejm) etc; and l/c when it is only a mooted body, such as the English parliament. Also, l/c **parliamentary**, even in parliamentary private secretary (abbreviated PPS) because there are many of them; but note Parliamentary Labour Party (PLP), of which there is one, and similarly Parliamentary Ombudsman. *See* PLP, ombudsman, and Politics special section (page 131)

Parliamentary Commissioner for Standards (caps) the post created in the light of the Nolan Committee on Standards in Public Life. He must *not* be referred to as the Parliamentary Ombudsman, who is the Parliamentary Commissioner for Administration. *See* ombudsman

partially, partly partially is of degree, eg, partially deaf; partly is of extension, eg, partly under water

participles beware the grammar trap of the disconnected (or unrelated) participle; eg, "Judging by the lingering camera shots, X's luck was not about to change" is wrong – the present participle *judging* has to have a following noun or pronoun in agreement (in other words, X's luck is not doing the judging). So the sentence has to be rephrased, as "Judging by the lingering camera shots, I saw that X's luck ...", or "To judge from the lingering camera shots, X's luck ..."

parties (political) Labour Party, Conservative Party, or any other party, with cap; also overseas, such as Republican Party, Democratic Party (though usually Republicans and Democrats will suffice). *See* Tory, and Politics special section (page 131)

part-time, part-timer (hyphens)

partygoer. *See* -goer

Pashtuns, biggest ethnic group in Afghanistan; the language is **Pashto**. *See* War on Terror

Passchendaele

passer-by, passers-by

past use rather than *last* in such phrases as "the past two weeks". *See* last

pastime

past tense of verbs almost always prefer the shorter form using final -*t* where appropriate; eg, **spelt** not spelled, **dreamt** not dreamed (though *never* earnt for earned)

pâté. *See* accents

Patient's Charter

Patriarch Aleksiy II (not Aleksei), head of the Russian Orthodox Church

PAYE (caps for pay as you earn)

Paymaster General

payout, **payoff** (no hyphens)

Peace Implementation Council in the former Yugoslavia. *See* Contact Group

peacekeeping, **peacemaking** etc (no hyphens)

peal of bells, **peel** of an orange etc

Pearl Harbor (not Harbour)

pedal as in bicycle; **peddle** as in selling drugs or advocating ideas. Thus a **pedaller** is someone who pedals a bike; a **pedlar** is the (often shady) small trader; and a drug-pusher is a **peddler**

pedalo (not pedallo), plural pedalos

peers a peer or a peeress has a seat in the House of Lords. A female life peer is a peeress usually referred to as Baroness Smith. After the first mention of the Marquess of Paddington, Earl of Euston, Viscount Pimlico or Lord Holborn, call them all Lord Paddington, Lord Euston etc. *See* Titles special section (page 171)

Peirce, Gareth, the human rights lawyer, is female

pejorative (not perjorative)

Peking only in phrases such as Peking duck or Peking man. The city is now **Beijing**. Note **pekinese** dogs. *See* Chinese names

Peloponnese

PEN, International the world association of writers

peninsula never *peninsular* when used as a noun; peninsular is the adjective, as in the **Peninsular War**

pension funds (not pensions funds, as plural)

pensioners take care with this word. Some readers take exception to "ambiguous" usage, so it should strictly be confined to people drawing their state pension (men at 65, women at 60). If in doubt, write **the elderly**, or as last resort, **senior citizen**. *See* elderly

peony (not paeony)

people use rather than *persons* wherever appropriate; exceptions would be "the law is no respecter of persons" or the ubiquitous *missing persons*. Take care with the apostrophe: remember that people is a plural, so the normal use is apostrophe "s", eg, "it is the people's wish"; very occasionally, *peoples* in the sense of *races* can take an "s" apostrophe, eg, "the African peoples' common heritage"

Pep, Peps not usually necessary to spell out as *personal equity plan* any more

Pepsi-Cola (hyphen, as Coca-Cola)

per try to avoid in phrases such as "six times per year"; "six times a year" is better

per cent always takes figures rather than the word, eg, 3 per cent, not three per cent. Usually use decimals rather than fractions (3.25 per cent rather than $3^1/_4$ per cent). Use % sign in headlines, never pc, and spell out per cent in text

percentage, proportion do not use as a synonym of *part* or *many* if that is all they mean in a sentence; eg, instead of "a large percentage of parents objected" say "many parents objected"

percentage points take care. If the mortgage rate rises from 8 per cent to 10 per cent, it does not rise by 2 per cent, but by two percentage points. Similarly if a political party's support drops from 50 per cent to 40 per cent in an opinion poll, it has lost ten percentage points or 20 per cent of its support

perestroika (not italics)

performance-related pay

Performing Right Society (not Rights)

Pergau dam (in Malaysia)

Persia use Iran for the modern state, and never Persian Gulf except in historical context. *See* Gulf

Personal Investment Authority (PIA), not *Investments*, has been subsumed into the **Financial Services Authority** (FSA)

personnel prefer *people* or *employees* or *workers* wherever possible

Perspex is a trade name, so must cap

Peterhouse, the Cambridge college, never takes College after the name. Neither does Christ Church, Oxford; nor do any Oxford or Cambridge colleges ending with Hall, eg, Lady Margaret Hall. Nor do Queen Mary and Royal Holloway at London University. *See* Cambridge, London, Oxford university entries

petfood (no hyphen); similarly, **catfood**, **dogfood**

phalangist (in Lebanon). *See* falangist

Pharaoh (not -oah), **pharaonic** (adjective l/c)

phenomenon, plural phenomena: beware the use of *phenomenal* as a cliché meaning remarkable or big

Phillips (no apostrophe), the auction house – still known as Phillips despite recent (summer 2002) on-off merger activity; but note **Philips**, the Dutch electronics company

phoney (not phony)

phosphorus (noun), but **phosphorous**, **phosphoric** (adjectives); **phosphorescence**

photo-finish, but **photo call** (two words); likewise, **photo opportunity**

photofit (l/c), but Identikit (cap)

Picketts Lock in North London (no apostrophe)

pidgin English (not pigeon)

piecemeal, **piecework**

pigeonhole(d) (do not hyphenate)

pigheaded

Pigott-Smith, Tim (not Piggott), actor, but **Lester Piggott** (jockey)

pilgrims are l/c, but the Pilgrim Fathers; note *The Pilgrim's Progress*

Pill, the (contraceptive), but **morning-after pill** (l/c)

Pimm's (the drink)

PIN (not Pin), abbreviation for personal identification number. Do not write PIN number, which is a tautology

pinstripes (-d)

pitbull (terrier)

pitstop (motor racing)

PKK, the Kurdish Workers' Party (not Kurdistan ...)

place names refer to the *Bartholomew Gazetteer* for place names in England, Wales and Scotland, and *The Times Atlas of the World* for the rest of the world. But there are exceptions; beware the new Welsh county names, and *see* unitary authorities, foreign places and Spanish regions

place name constructions two ugly devices to avoid are, eg, a *Gosport, Hampshire, housewife*, and *Manchester's Piccadilly station*; say instead *a housewife from Gosport, Hampshire*, and *Piccadilly station, Manchester*

Plaid Cymru (the Welsh Nationalist Party)

plane, on a higher (not plain)

planes always prefer *aircraft* or *jets* (where applicable). Avoid *airplanes*. *See* aircraft

Play-Doh (proprietary)

play-off

plays titles in italics. *See* Arts special section (page 18)

PlayStation

plc (all l/c) can usually be dropped from company names. *See* Ltd

PLP, the Parliamentary Labour Party. *See* Politics special section (page 131)

plurals make corporate bodies and institutions singular unless this looks odd. Thus "The National Trust is ...", but sports teams are plural, eg, "Arsenal were worth their 8-0 lead".

Whether singular or plural, always maintain consistency within a story

plus, **minus** do not use as variants of *and* or *without*

Poe, Edgar Allan

point-to-point

poetess avoid (say poet). *See* feminine designations

Poet Laureate (caps); plural is Poets Laureate

poetry or blank verse quotes spacing should be as follows around the slash to separate the lines: The play's the thing/ Wherein I'll catch the conscience of the king

Polaroid is a trade name, so must cap

Polgar, Judit. *See* chess names

police forces cap the word Police when it is part of the full name of the force. This applies to the following forces: Metropolitan Police, City of London Police, British Transport Police, Ministry of Defence Police, Bedfordshire Police, Cleveland Police, Dorset Police (Force), Essex Police, Greater Manchester Police, Humberside Police, Kent Police, Lincolnshire Police, Merseyside Police, Northamptonshire Police, Northumbria Police, North Yorkshire Police, South Yorkshire Police, Staffordshire Police, Surrey Police, Sussex Police, Thames Valley Police, West Midlands Police, West Yorkshire Police, Dyfed–Powys Police, North Wales Police, Central Scotland Police, Grampian Police, Lothian and Borders Police, Strathclyde Police, Tayside Police. Other forces use Constabulary instead of Police (eg, Cambridgeshire Constabulary, Hertfordshire Constabulary), so either give that full title or, more commonly, say Cambridgeshire police, Hertfordshire police etc. Do not cap when referring to a local division, eg, Luton police, or police in Luton. If in doubt, consult *Whitaker's Almanack* under "Police Authorities"

policemen take care with this word. Certain senior officers, men and women, regularly chide us for using *policemen* when we mean *police officers*. If in doubt, use the latter (PC in every sense)

police ranks wherever possible outside lists, avoid the inelegant abbreviated forms such as Det Con, Det Chief Insp. Spell out, even if inconvenient sometimes. An exception is PC, or WPC (for Woman Police Constable). PC is also acceptable in headlines. Compound titles do not take hyphens in the police force. Detective Sergeant X becomes Sergeant X after the first mention. Inspector and all ranks above are usually Mr after the first mention. *See* Chief Constable

Police Staff College, at Bramshill,

Hampshire; or simply the police college (l/c), Bramshill

policyholder, **policymaker**, but policy document

Politburo (usually cap)

Pope, the not usually necessary to give his full name, eg, Pope John Paul II (unless several Popes are mentioned in a story), but always cap. Note **papacy**, **pontiff** (l/c). *See* Churches special section (page 37)

poppadum

populist should not be confused with, or used as a synonym of, popular; it means supporting the interest of ordinary people, or pandering to mass public taste

Porritt, Jonathon despite his baronetcy, he prefers not to use Sir

Portakabin (cap), trade name

possibly like most qualifiers, this word can (usually) be omitted

postal addresses in news and features, prefer to say Bromley, southeast London (rather than Kent), and Kingston upon Thames, southwest London (rather than Surrey) etc. This leaves the old counties such as Middlesex to be used principally in their historical or sporting contexts. Also avoid the clumsy possessive form such as Manchester's Moss Side, London's East End; say Moss Side, Manchester, the East End of London. There is no

need to use postcodes except when giving an address for information. *See* addresses

postcode (no hyphen)

Postcomm, the postal regulator. *See* Post Office, regulators

postgraduate, **undergraduate** (noun and adjective both one word)

Post-it Notes (proprietary, cap P and N)

Post-Modern (caps, hyphen). *See* artistic movements

post mortem wherever possible write *post-mortem examination* in reports, though *post mortem* is acceptable nowadays in headlines

Post Office will no longer be called Consignia (late 2002), but is being renamed Royal Mail Group, one of whose trading subsidiaries is **Post Office Ltd** (or the **Post Office**, colloquially), which runs the big urban post offices. Other subsidiaries are **Parcelforce Worldwide** (parcels delivery) and **Royal Mail** (post delivery). Note l/c post office for the branches, sub-post office, sub-postmaster, sub-postmistress. *See* Consignia

postwar, **prewar** (adjectives, commonly referring to the Second World War). Do not use adverbially (as in "there were a million unemployed prewar")

potatoes (plural, as tomatoes)

POLITICS

GENERAL POINTS

Always check the spelling of MPs and their constituencies if not entirely familiar: the best reference is *The Times Guide to the House of Commons*. Similarly, check *Vacher's Parliamentary Companion* or *Who's Who* for peers. For guidance on when to cap or l/c Government, Opposition, Parliament, Party, see individual entries in the alphabetical list of this Style Guide.

Remember that Government, Cabinet, Opposition, Parliament, Party etc take the singular verb, eg, the Cabinet is considering . . .

It is never necessary to say *Tony Blair, the Prime Minister*, etc: we may assume that *Times* readers know who the Prime Minister is. But it may be helpful to the flow of the story to write, eg, *the Prime Minister said . . .* lower down the story, to avoid the endless repetition of *Mr Blair*.

PARLIAMENTARY STYLES

Act(s) always capped, whether fully identified or not

backbench (adjective), **backbenchers**, but **the back benches**; similarly, **frontbench** (adj), but **the front bench**; and **crossbench** (in the Lords), **the cross benches**

Bill(s) always capped (as with Acts above). Bills are read a first time without a debate. The second reading debate is the debate on the principle of the Bill. The Bill then goes to its committee stage, usually in a standing committee composed of about 20 MPs, but occasionally on the floor of the Commons. It then returns to the Commons chamber for its report stage and third reading, which is the final debate on the principle of the Bill. It then goes to the Lords, where similar procedures apply. Note that some legislation starts in the Lords and comes to the Commons thereafter

Cabinet always capped (as with Act and Bill), whether used as a noun or adjectivally, except in the informal **kitchen cabinet**. **Cabinet committees** should be capped

chamber (l/c)

Clause Four (as in Labour Party policy); but Clause 4 permissible in headlines

closure, as in *move the closure*

committees cap **select committees** when full title, such as the Select Committee on the Environment; Cabinet committees such as the **Cabinet Committee** on the Intelligence Services; the **Public Accounts Committee** (PAC); the **1922 Committee** (of Tory backbenchers); the **National Executive Committee** (NEC) of the Labour Party (or *Labour's national executive* as a shorter alternative)

Conservative Central Office, second mention Central Office (never CCO)

crossbench, the cross benches (*see* backbench above)

Cunningham through common usage, refer to him at first mention as Jack Cunningham (rather than John), then Dr Cunningham (though he is not a medical doctor)

deputy speakers there are three, and should appear thus: John Jones, the Deputy Speaker

dispatch box (l/c)

Downing Street policy unit; **10 Downing Street**, or **No 10**

Duncan Smith, Iain (no hyphen)

early day motion (l/c)

elections general election *always* l/c; similarly **by-election, European elections** etc

frontbench (adjective), **the front bench** (*see* backbench above)

galleries l/c, but the **Press Gallery**, **Strangers' Gallery** etc

group cap in cases such as the **92 Group** (of Tory rightwingers)

guillotine (l/c, no quotation marks)

Hansard (italics)

House of Lords officers the Clerk of the Parliaments, the Clerk Assistant (of the Parliaments), the Reading Clerk (of the House of Lords)

leaders Leader of the House, **Leader of the Opposition** (caps in both cases), but the Conservative/Labour/Liberal Democrat leader (l/c), the leader of the party etc

Liberal Democrats permissible to use Lib Dems in either headlines or text (though sparingly in text). The term *Liberals* must not be used as a synonym of Liberal Democrats

Lower House (caps)

Members of Parliament Member is capped; in almost every case, MPs is the preferable form. But in the Political Sketch, and discursive or commentary articles, the term Members sometimes occurs for stylistic reasons and should be retained and capped; similarly in such articles, the Member for Billericay etc, the Hon Member, and so on

National Executive Committee (NEC) of the Labour Party, or simply Labour's national executive

new Labour l/c "n", quotes not usually necessary, except when the writer or speaker is making a particular, perhaps ironic, point. But keep caps in slogans such as "New Labour, New Danger", and note New Deal

1922 Committee of Tory backbenchers

Oath of Allegiance (caps), the oath thereafter

one member, one vote (no hyphens)

One Nation Tories, One Nation politics etc

Opposition the same cap or l/c rules apply as to Government – cap as a noun but generally l/c as adjective, eg, "He accused the Opposition of lying", but "He said it was an opposition lie"

order, order paper (l/c)

Parliament cap always in the British context (but see in alphabetical list for when to cap foreign parliaments). The cap rule now applies even to phrases such as the *lifetime of this Parliament* or the *Bill is unlikely to progress until the next Parliament*. The adjective **parliamentary** is usually l/c except when used as part of a title, eg, Parliamentary Labour Party (PLP)

parliamentary private secretary (l/c), abbreviated **PPS**

Part I, Part II of a Bill etc; caps also with **Section 2, Article 8** etc

party abbreviations in lists or political sketches or reports of debates where party affiliation is added after an MP's name – eg, Hilary Benn (Lab, Leeds Central) – use Lab for Labour, C for Conservative (not Con), and LD for Liberal Democrat (not Lib Dem)

party conference l/c conference, as in Labour Party conference

Private Member's Bill (caps)

Public Accounts Committee (PAC)

Queen's Speech (caps)

Question Time, **Prime Minister's Questions**, also Agriculture Questions, Treasury Questions etc; but **questions** (l/c) to the Prime Minister, the Foreign Secretary etc

Register of Members' Interests (caps)

Royal Assent (caps)

royal commissions. *See* in main alphabetical list

select committees cap when giving full title, eg, Treasury Select Committee

Serjeant at Arms

Smith the widow of John Smith is Baroness Smith of Gilmorehill (thereafter Lady Smith); she is *not* Dame Elizabeth Smith

Speaker usual style is *Michael Martin, the Speaker*, at first mention, thereafter *the Speaker* or *Mr Martin*

spin-doctor (hyphen)

State Opening (of Parliament) (caps)

Tea Room two words with initial caps, in Commons Tea Room

ten-minute rule (Bill etc)

Treasury bench

Upper House (caps)

Vote (of money) takes cap

West Lothian question (l/c "q")

whips cap for the **Chief Whip**, **Opposition Chief Whip**, **Whips' Office**; but l/c as in **three-line whip**, **he lost the party whip**, **a government whip**

Woolsack (initial cap)

pothole (as in caving or road surfaces), **potholer**

pound do not use the £ by itself, except in headlines

PoW (prisoner of war); plural PoWs

Powell, General Colin (keep the General despite his civilian political status)

Powergen, no longer PowerGen

PPE the university degree is philosophy, politics and economics (not politics, philosophy etc)

PPP. *See* Private Finance Initiative

practical, **practicable** do not confuse. Practical means adapted to actual conditions or (of a person) able to make things function well; practicable means capable of being effected or accomplished

practice (noun); **practise** (verb). It is an inexcusable practice for sub-editors to confuse the two; writers should practise getting it right

Prado gallery, Madrid. *See* Pardo

praying mantis (not preying)

praesidium, not presidium

prearrange

Pre-Budget Report (initial caps)

predilection (not predeliction)

pre-empt

pregnant avoid the infelicitous phrase *she fell pregnant*

Premier do not use in text as a synonym of Prime Minister, though very occasionally its use in the headline of a foreign story (never British) may be permitted. Generally, confine the word to heads of government of the Canadian provinces or Australian states, when it should take a cap. Premiership is preferable to prime-ministership

premiere, of a play, ballet etc (no accent)

Premiership (football) refer to the Barclaycard Premiership (no longer Carling) at first mention, the Premiership thereafter, for the top division in English football; the organisation that runs it is the FA Premier League. Take care not to confuse the competition and the organisation. Similarly, the lower divisions form the Nationwide League, first division, second division (note l/c) etc; this competition is run by the Football League. *See* Sports special section (page 160)

premise is an assumption in an argument; **premises** (property) take the plural verb, eg, "the premises are well positioned"

Premium Bonds (caps)

prepositional verbs avoid wherever possible. Examples such as *measure up to, get on with* are acceptable on the odd occasion. Others such as *consult with, meet with* (where the preposition is tautologous) are hideous and must never be used

Pre-Raphaelite. *See* artistic movements

Presbyterian beware, especially with the adjective Scots. *See* Church, and Churches special section (page 37)

present better than *current* but often redundant

President (of any country, also **President of the European Commission**), cap at first and all subsequent mentions; but l/c **presidency** (as in the French presidency of the EU). Also note that **presidents of companies or organisations** will normally take l/c, though this rule should be relaxed for leading national organisations, such as **President of the Law Society** and **President of the TUC**

press always l/c except in titles such as the Press Complaints Commission. *See* broadsheet

prestigious try to avoid this much overworked word and find an appropriate substitute such as *highly regarded, admired, eminent, esteemed, leading, noted, outstanding, powerful* etc

Pret A Manger (restaurants), no accents, cap A

pretension, but **pretentious**

prevaricate must not be confused

with **procrastinate**. The first means to speak or act evasively; the second to defer action, to be dilatory

preventive (not preventative)

PricewaterhouseCoopers (PwC for short), the merged accountants

prime meridian (l/c)

Prime Minister cap for every country. But l/c when referring to an unspecific, eg, "he would make a good prime minister". Never say, eg, Prime Minister Tony Blair or even Tony Blair, the Prime Minister (*Times* readers will know who Mr Blair is); say instead Tony Blair at first mention, then the Prime Minister at next mention. Never use *Premier* for the British Prime Minister, and never use PM except sparingly in headlines. *See* Premier

primeval

Prince avoid the familiar forms of Prince Charles and Prince Philip at least until they have been given their full designation of Prince of Wales and Duke of Edinburgh; even then, prefer the Prince and the Duke at subsequent mentions. Note **The Prince's Trust**. *See* royal, Royal Family

Princess of Wales. *See* Diana, Princess of Wales

Princes Street, Edinburgh

principal (noun or adjective) means chief, main, important, head etc; eg, the principal of a college, or the team's principal objective. It must never be confused with **principle**, which is a noun meaning concept, ideal, rule, moral etc; eg, her Christian principles

Principality, the cap in Welsh context

printout

prior to avoid wherever possible; use *before*

prise apart (not prize)

Prison Service (caps); **Prisons Board** (caps and note "s"); **Director-General of the Prison Service** (caps); **Chief Inspector of Prisons** (caps). *See* Governor, Probation Service

prison visitors be careful to differentiate clearly between two groups of prison visitors; these are:

a. members of the National Association of Prison Visitors, who visit prisoners in the "social" sense of visiting; and

b. members of prison boards of visitors, who visit as watchdogs in an official role and sometimes make recommendations on matters such as discipline and security

Pritt Stik (initial caps)

Private Finance Initiative (PFI), sometimes now known as **Public Private Partnerships** (initial caps)

private sector, public sector do not use hyphens even when employed adjectivally, eg, public sector pay (as high street shopping)

privatised industries. *See* regulators

Privy Council, but **Privy Counsellors** (not Councillors)

prize-money (use hyphen)

prizewinner (one word); a Nobel prizewinner (unspecific Nobel award), but winner of the Nobel Prize for Literature (a specific award); also, a Nobel prize-winning novel. *See* Nobel

Probation Service (caps, as Prison Service)

probe use only in a scientific, medical or space context. Never to be used as *inquiry*, even in headlines

problem be sparing with use of this overworked word

procrastinate means to defer action, to be dilatory. *See* prevaricate

Procter & Gamble (-er and ampersand)

Procurator Fiscal, Crown prosecutor in Scotland. *See* Courts special section (page 47)

profanities. *See* obscenities, four-letter words

Professor of History, Psychology etc (caps when given as specific designation after a name); thereafter, the professor or Professor X. *See* university posts

proffer, proffered; not profer, proferred

profits, especially in Business stories, should always state the basis of the figure (pre-tax, operating etc)

program (computers); programme (the arts etc)

pro-life beware this contentious phrase for the anti-abortion lobby (especially in US context); use the phrase **anti-abortion** wherever possible, but when "pro-life" is unavoidable always quote it

Proms, acceptable abbreviation of Promenade Concerts; **Promenaders**; and the **Last Night of the Proms**

prone means lying face-down; **supine**, face-up

propeller (not -or)

prophecy (noun), **prophesy** (verb)

proportion. *See* percentage

pros and cons

protagonist means a supporter (of either side) in a debate or quarrel; it does not mean advocate or proponent

protégé

protester (*never* -or); but *see* demonstrator

Protestant beware of using for all Christians who are not Roman Catholic. *See* Churches special section (page 37)

proven *not proven* is the Scottish legal verdict. In general use, prefer *proved* to *proven*; but *proven* and *unproven* may be used as a colloquial alternative

provided that (not *providing that*)

Province, the. *See* Ireland (paragraph d)

provinces, provincial take great care of these words in the context of "outside London". Many regard them as patronising; use *the regions* or *regional* wherever possible

prurient means having an unhealthy obsession with sex; it does *not* mean puritanical

PSBR, the public sector borrowing requirement

public house pub is fully acceptable in text or headlines

public interest immunity certificate (abbreviate to PIIC, or simply *the certificate*)

publicly (never publically)

Public Record Office (not Records)

public school independent school is now a preferable term; say public schoolboys, public schoolgirls, if we have to use the phrase

public sector. *See* private sector

Puffa jacket (must cap P, trademark); use padded or quilted jacket as the generic

Pulitzer prizes. *See* Nobel for when to cap

pullout (noun, one word); but *to pull out*

punctuation some important reminders:

a. Commas: keep commas inside quotes in the following type of "broken" sentence: "The trouble is," he said, "that this is a contentious issue." Omit the comma before *if, unless, before, since, when* unless the rhythm or sense of the sentence demands it. Avoid the so-called *Oxford comma*; say "he ate bread, butter and jam" rather than "he ate bread, butter, and jam"

b. Dashes: should not be used in place of commas. Too many dashes can be ugly and disruptive

c. Note that **punctuation marks** go inside the inverted commas if they relate to the words quoted, outside if they relate to the main sentence, eg, She is going to classes in "health and beauty". If the whole sentence is a quotation, the final point goes inside, eg, "Beauty is truth, truth beauty."

d. Interrogation marks are never used with indirect questions or

rhetorical questions, eg, "She asked why he did not laugh."

e. Parentheses should be used sparingly; try to use commas instead

f. *And* and *but*, both **conjunctions**, may occasionally be used at the beginning of a sentence, especially for emphasis

g. With **ellipses**, use three points with full space after last word, then thin-spacing between points, then full space before next word; for example, *not only . . . but also*

puns an enjoyable device for headline writers. Restrict their use to funny or light stories or features and if in doubt, avoid; but if irresistible, make sure they are in good taste

Puritan do not use the word for the 16th/17th-century religious group as a contemporary adjective; puritanical is just permitted

putsch, a military seizure of power, as in coup

pygmy, pygmies

Pyramids the three main Pyramids at Giza (including the Great Pyramid) should be capped. But there are many other pyramids (l/c) throughout Egypt

pyrrhic (as with victory), l/c

Q

Qantas (not *Quantas*)

qat rather than kat or khat, the hypnotic drug

, QC, MP, commas each side when used after name

QCA, the Qualifications and Curriculum Authority; should be spelt out at first mention. It is an amalgamation (from autumn 1997) of the National Council for Vocational Qualifications and the School Curriculum and Assessment Authority

QE2 normally spell out *Queen Elizabeth 2* at first mention, thereafter *QE2* or simply *the ship*. Do not describe her as a liner (say *cruise ship*). *See* liner

Qom (not Qum), Iranian city

quadriplegia, **quadriplegic** (not quadra-)

quality press prefer *broadsheet*. *See* broadsheet

quango (short for quasi-autonomous non-governmental organisation), no need to spell out or to quote

quantum leap avoid this cliché wherever possible

quarter sessions, like assizes, no

longer function, having been replaced by the Crown Court

Quebeckers, rather than *Québecois*

Queen, the note the Queen's Speech (to Parliament), caps; also the Queen's Birthday Honours. NB: the Queen is not "introduced" to people; people are introduced, or (even more correctly) presented, to the Queen. *See* Royal Family, New Year Honours

Queen Elizabeth the Queen Mother (no commas); at first mention now write **the late Queen Elizabeth the Queen Mother**, thereafter the Queen Mother

Queen Elizabeth II Conference Centre, London (not QE2 or any other variant)

Queens, New York

Queensberry, Marquess of, and Queensberry Rules

Queen's Club

Queens' College, Cambridge, but **The Queen's College, Oxford** (*see* Cambridge and Oxford); **Queen's University Belfast** (but in formal contexts, The Queen's University of Belfast) – and either form can be shortened to Queen's Belfast

Queens Park Rangers (thereafter QPR)

queueing (with middle "e")

questionnaire

Question Time, **Prime Minister's Questions** (caps), but **questions** (l/c) to the Prime Minister, Foreign Secretary etc. *See* Politics special section (page 131)

quicker never use as an adverb – always say *more quickly*. Quicker must be confined to adjectival comparison, eg, "he started at a quicker pace"

quid pro quo (not italic)

quiz show, as chat show, game show, talk show etc (no hyphen)

quotation marks (inverted commas) remember, **single quotes in headlines, straps and standfirsts; double quotes in captions**.

The only other use for single inverted commas is quotations within quotations. Avoid inverted commas in sentences where they are clearly unnecessary, eg, *He described the attack as "outrageous"*.

Quotation marks are no longer to be used for works of art.

See inverted commas, italics. *See also* punctuation (paragraph c) for when punctuation goes inside or outside quotation marks

quotes direct quotes should be corrected only to remove the solecisms and other errors that occur in speech but look silly in print. Always take care that quotes are correctly attributed; and especially that literary or biblical quotations are 100 per cent accurate

R

race references to race should be used only when relevant to the sense of the story. The word is often better replaced by *people*, *nation*, *group* etc

racecourse, **racehorse**, **racetrack**. *See* horse race and Sports special section (page 160)

racked by doubts, pain etc; not *wracked*

racket for tennis, not racquet. The game is also rackets

RADA (all caps), the Royal Academy of Dramatic Art

radio compounds are hyphenated in the wireless context (eg, **radio-telephone**); but one word when they concern rays (eg, **radioactive**, **radioisotope**, **radiotherapy**). Broadcasting frequencies are measured in megahertz (MHz) and kilohertz (kHz)

radio ham this term should strictly be applied only to licensed amateur radio operators, who are offended when it is used to apply to unlicensed "eavesdroppers" spying on private phone calls etc. Take care

Radio 1, 2, 3, 4, Radio 5 Live; Classic FM, BBC Radio, talkSPORT, Jazz FM etc. But with foreign stations, usually l/c, eg, Israel radio, Haiti radio, Moscow radio, Singapore radio etc; cap only if we know it is the specific name of the station or organisation

RAF crews went on **operations** (or ops) in the Second World War; American (USAF) crews went on **missions**. Do not confuse

RAF Regiment is a Corps within the Royal Air Force

railways write **East Coast Main Line**, **West Coast Main Line**, **Channel Tunnel Rail Link** (now all initial caps). *See* train companies

rainforest (one word)

raison d'être (use italics)

Raleigh, Sir Walter (not Ralegh)

R&B abbreviation for rhythm and blues

ranging from overworked and often unnecessary phrase. There must be a scale in which the elements might be ranged: "ranging from 15 to 25 years" is correct, "a crowd ranging from priests to golfers" is not

ranks. *See* Armed Forces special section (page 14), police ranks

Ranks Hovis McDougall, but (The) Rank Organisation

Rann of Kutch (prefer to Kachchh), area on India-Pakistan border

Rapid Reaction Force cap in Nato context as the force already exists, but l/c in European army context until it is made official – or not

rarefied, rarefy (not rarified)

rateable

rave acceptable in context as a musical event. *See* gig

razzmatazz

re- whenever possible, run the prefix on to the word it qualifies, eg, readmission, remake, rework, etc; but there are two main classes of exceptions:

a. where the word after re- begins with an "e", eg, re-election, re-emerge, re-examine, re-enter etc

b. where there could be serious ambiguity in compounds such as re-creation (recreation), re-cover (recover), re-dress (redress). *See* hyphens

realpolitik (not italic)

rebut means to argue to the contrary, producing evidence; to **refute** is to win such an argument. Neither should be used as a synonym of *reject* or *deny*, both of which are good, straightforward words. Nor should they be used for *dispute* or *respond to*

receive "receiving an injury" is to be discouraged, though not banned. Prefer to say *sustained* or *suffered*; and never say someone received a broken leg etc – prefer suffered a broken leg or, better still, broke a leg. *See* injure

reckless (as synonym for rash or foolhardy); not *wreckless*

record never say "set a new record", "was an all-time record" etc, where both qualifiers are tautologous

recorders for when to cap, *see* Courts special section (page 47)

recrudescence do not confuse with *resurgence* or *revival*. It means worsening, in the sense of reopening wounds or recurring diseases

redbrick (university), but a **red-brick** building

Red Planet (caps), informal name for Mars

referendum, plural referendums, as with conundrums, stadiums, forums and most words ending in -um. But note millennia, strata

refute take care with this word. *See* rebut

Regent's Park

regimen should be restricted to medical contexts – a prescribed course of exercise, way of life, diet etc. Do not use as a synonym of **regime** (government or administrative contexts)

register office, not registry office

Register of Members' Interests
(caps). *See* Politics special section
(page 131)

Registrar (Oxford), but
Registrary (Cambridge)

Registrar-General

regulators of the privatised utilities
and other watchdogs should be
styled as follows:

a. **DWI** – the **Drinking Water
   Inspectorate** regulates public
   water supplies in England and
   Wales. It has a chief inspector

b. **Ofcom** – the **Office of
   Communications** is a new
   super-regulator being set up (mid-
   2002) incorporating, and replacing,
   the Office of Telecommunications
   (Oftel), the Broadcasting Standards
   Commission, the Independent
   Television Commission, the Radio
   Authority and the
   Radiocommunications Agency. It
   is due to come into operation in
   2003, and will have a chairman

c. **Ofgem** – the **Office of Gas
   and Electricity Markets**,
   replacing the former Offer and
   Ofgas. The energy regulator is
   replaced by a regulatory authority,
   the **Gas and Electricity
   Markets Authority**, which has a
   chairman (no longer a director-
   general) who is also chief
   executive of Ofgem

d. **Ofsted** – the **Office for**

Standards in Education,
officially the Office of Her
Majesty's Inspector of Schools in
England

e. **Ofwat** – the **Office of Water
   Services** has a director-general
   and regulates water and sewerage
   companies in England and Wales

f. **Office of Fair Trading** – the
   OFT. The *consumer watchdog* can
   be used as an alternative; it has a
   director-general

g. **Postcomm** – the **Postal
   Services Commission** has a
   chief executive. It regulates the
   postal service and Consignia/
   Royal Mail/Post Office

h. **Rail Regulator** – the **Office of
   the Rail Regulator** – this one
   capped as it is the official title.
   Changes in the Transport Act
   2000 confirm the Rail Regulator
   as an economic regulator

i. **SRA** – the **Strategic Rail
   Authority** since February 2001
   has responsibility for developing
   the rail network and encouraging
   integration. Subsuming the powers
   of the Office of Passenger Rail
   Franchising (Opraf) and the
   British Railways Board (BRB), it
   is a strategic investor, awarder of
   passenger rail franchises and
   enforcer of consumer protection

Reith Lecture(s)

reject. *See* rebut

relatively. *See* comparatively

Religious Right (caps) in American politics. *See* Right

remainder avoid as a synonym of *the rest*

REME, the Royal Electrical and Mechanical Engineers (never Reme). *See* Armed Forces special section (page 14)

Remembrance Sunday (preferred to Day)

Renaissance, the; but l/c renaissance as synonym of *revival* or *rebirth*

reorganise

repellent (noun or adjective, not repellant)

replacements in rugby union, not substitutes. *See* Sports special section (page 160)

report l/c in titles of official documents such as Taylor report

reportedly avoid this slack word, which suggests that the writer is unsure of the source of the material

Republic of Ireland, or Irish Republic. *See* Ireland

republican l/c except when in an official name, such as the Republican Party or Republicans in the US. *See* Ireland

rerun

Resolution cap in context of UN, eg, Resolution 688

respect of avoid "in respect of" whenever possible; never say "in respect to"

responsible people bear responsibility, things do not. Storms are not responsible for damage; they cause it. Avoid the phrase "the IRA *claimed responsibility* for the bombing"; say instead "the IRA admitted causing the bombing"

restaurateur (never restauranteur)

result in avoid this lazy phrase and always find an alternative, such as *cause, bring, create, evoke, lead to* etc

re-use one of the re- words where the hyphen is essential as *reuse* is hideous

Reuters use this form now in every context (no longer Reuter)

Reveille, like Last Post, is sounded, not played

Revelation, Book of (not Revelations)

reverend at first mention, the style is "the Rev Tom Jones", then Mr Jones. *Never* say "the Rev Jones" or (even worse) "Rev Jones" (which is as great a solecism as calling Sir Bobby Charlton "Sir Charlton"). A parson and his wife are referred to as "the Rev Tom and Mrs Jones". *See* archbishops, Churches special section (page 37)

Review takes the cap in names of government programmes, such as

Strategic Defence Review, Comprehensive Spending Review etc

Reykjavik, Iceland

rhinoceroses (plural)

Rhodes scholar/scholarship (l/c "s")

Rhys-Jones, Sophie now the Countess of Wessex (subsequent mentions the Countess). *See* Titles special section (page 171)

RIBA (all caps), abbreviation of the Royal Institute of British Architects

Richter scale measures the energy released by an earthquake. It runs from 0 to 8; say "the earthquake measured 6 on the Richter scale"

RICS, Royal Institution of Chartered Surveyors (note all caps, and Institution)

riffle, riffling, as in flicking through papers or clothes on a rail; rifling only in the sense of ransacking

Right, the cap in the political context when referring to a group of like-minded individuals, eg, "The Right added to John Major's dilemma on the EU"; but l/c in "the party swung to the right". When the Right is qualified, generally keep the adjective l/c, eg, the far Right (but note the Religious Right in the US). Also, the **right wing, right-wing contenders, rightwingers**. *See* Left, Politics special section (page 131)

rigmarole (not rigamarole)

ring-fence (hyphen)

Rio Tinto no longer Rio Tinto-Zinc or RTZ

Riot Act (initial caps), as in "read the Riot Act"

rip off (verb), **rip-off** (noun or adj) avoid this cliché except in quotes such as "rip-off Britain"

Rise, the Channel 4 breakfast TV programme; do not use *RI:SE*

riverbank (one word)

rivers cap in context of River Thames, the Mississippi River (or simply the Thames, the Mississippi etc). Similarly, cap **estuary** when part of the name. *See* Thames

riveting try to avoid its clichéd use as a metaphor

roadblock, roadbuilding, roadbuilder etc

road rage no longer any need to quote, even at first mention

roads as tautologous to write "the M5 motorway" as "the A435 road", but correct to say "the M40 London to Birmingham motorway". Unnecessary to define the M25 as London's orbital motorway, but generally, define a road geographically unless context is clear

Robert the Bruce (prefer to Robert Bruce); subsequent mentions, the Bruce

rock'n'roll

Rohypnol must not be referred to as the "date rape drug"

Rollerblade is proprietary, so must be capped. The American company's lawyers insist that even Rollerblading takes the cap; use in-line skates/ skating instead

rollerskate, rollercoaster

roll-on, roll-off (as in ferries), abbreviated to ro-ro

rollover (as in Lotto, the renamed national lottery), no hyphen

Rolls-Royce

Roman Catholic. *See* Catholic

Romania, not Rumania. *See* Ceausescu

Roman numerals usually no full points; thus Edward VIII, Article XVI, Part II, Psalm xxiii. But in official documents, to designate sub-sections, use the points, eg, i., ii., iv., etc

roofs (not rooves)

rooms say living room, drawing room, laundry room (no hyphens except when adjectival, eg, living-room carpet), but bathroom, bedroom, tearoom

rottweiler (l/c). *See* dogs

round-up (hyphenate as noun)

row be sparing in the use of this word, especially in headlines.

Alternatives are *rift, split, clash* etc, and *dispute* in text. However, row is not banned

Rowntree be sure to distinguish between the Joseph Rowntree Foundation, a charity and independent funder of social policy research and development; and the Joseph Rowntree Reform Trust, not a charity and an entirely separate company that funds projects often with a political dimension

royal, royalty l/c for royalty but cap the Royal Family; royal is usually l/c when used adjectivally, as in royal baby, royal approval, the royal wave, but takes the cap in titles such as **Royal Assent, Royal Collection, Royal Household, Royal Yacht** etc

Royal & SunAlliance (note ampersand and SunAlliance)

Royal College of Nursing (not Nurses)

royal commissions should be capped when the full title is given, eg, the Royal Commission on Environmental Pollution, but otherwise l/c, the royal commission. NB: Royal Commission on Reform of the House of Lords. *See* committee

Royal Corps of Signals, or **Royal Signals** (not Royal Corps of Signallers). *See* Armed Forces special section (page 14)

Royal Family takes caps, British and overseas; with names of the British Royal Family, give fully at first mention, eg, the Duke of Edinburgh, thereafter the Duke (cap) or occasionally Prince Philip; Prince William, thereafter the Prince. In royalty context, the cap after first mention should be confined to the British Royal Family and overseas heads of state. *See* Queen, Duke, Prince, Diana, heads of state, Titles special section (page 171)

Royal Fine Art Commission

Royal Fleet Auxiliary ships are entitled RFA, not HMS; eg, *RFA Fort George*. *See* Armed Forces special section (page 14)

Royal Institute of International Affairs (often known as Chatham House); *not* Institution

Royal Military Academy Sandhurst; similarly, **Royal Air Force College Cranwell** and **Royal Naval College Dartmouth** (no commas)

Royal National Lifeboat Institution (RNLI); not Life-Boat

Royal Over-Seas League. *See* London clubs

Royal Shakespeare Company (thereafter the RSC), and **Royal Opera House** (ROH); but generally no need for the Royal with Albert Hall, Festival Hall, National Theatre

Royal Standard is only for the Sovereign. Other members of the Royal Family have a personal standard. *See* ensign

Royal Train caps, as with the Royal Yacht

Royal Welch Fusiliers, The; but Welsh Guards. *See* Armed Forces special section (page 14)

Royal Yacht Britannia, or the *Britannia*. She is now decommissioned, so refer to her as the former Royal Yacht

RPI, the retail prices index (note plural and l/c)

RPM (caps), resale price maintenance (not retail); and **rpm** (l/c), revolutions per minute

RSPCA does not exist in Scotland, which has the Scottish SPCA

rubbish do not use as a verb

Rubens, not Reubens (the Flemish painter)

Rubinstein, Arthur the late pianist preferred to be called Arthur rather than the oft-written Artur

Rue Royale. *See* French names

run-down (adjective), as in decaying or exhausted; **rundown** (noun) as in briefing; to **run down** (verb)

running-mate (hyphen)

Rural England Council for the Protection of Rural England (CPRE), *not* Preservation

rush hour (noun), but rush-hour (adjective, hyphen, as in rush-hour traffic)

rushed to hospital avoid this cliché. Say simply *taken to* or *driven to*; similarly, say a victim was *flown to hospital* rather than *airlifted to* ... Always avoid the American *hospitalise*

Russia take care not to designate parts of the former Soviet Union as Russia when they no longer are, eg, Ukraine, Georgia. The same applies to the people (though there are millions of ethnic Russians throughout the former Soviet Union). So always specify the republic concerned and do not use *Russian* in the inclusive sense except in the phrase *Russian vodka*. Use Soviet and the Soviet Union only in their historical contexts – and **avoid USSR** wherever possible. *See* Soviet

Russian names use "i" as first name ending, but "y" for surnames, eg, Arkadi Volsky, Gennadi Yavlinsky (but note the exception Rutskoi); and use "k" rather than "x" in the middle, eg, Aleksei, Aleksandr; also note Viktor. We should use the -ya rather than -ia in Natalya and Tatyana (not Natalia, Tatiana). But note that the styles of Garry Kasparov and Anatoly Karpov are sufficiently Westernised to be spelt thus. *See* chess names

S

saccharin (noun), **saccharine** (adjective)

sack avoid in the sense of *dismiss* except in headlines (and never say *axed* or *fired* in this context)

sacrilegious (from sacrilege; not sacreligious)

Saddam Hussein, President; full out first mention, then Saddam

Sadler's Wells

said prefer the construction *Mr Brown said* rather than *said Mr Brown*. *See* writes

Sainsbury the formal style is J Sainsbury (no point), especially in business stories, but Sainsbury's is permissible in general news stories. *See* initials

Saint is nearly always abbreviated to St

St Albans

St Andrews, the town and university in Fife

St Bride's, Fleet Street (not St Brides')

St Catharine's College, Cambridge, but **St Catherine's College**, Oxford. *See* Oxford, Cambridge, Catherine

St David's, Pembrokeshire, for the village, Cathedral and St David's Head, but the Bishop of St Davids does not take the apostrophe

St John's, Smith Square (use comma)

St Giles' Cathedral, Edinburgh

St Helens, Merseyside

St James's Palace. *See* Court of …

St John Ambulance Brigade/ Association

St John's, Newfoundland, but **Saint John**, New Brunswick

St John's Wood, London

St Katharine Docks, but St Katharine's Yacht Haven

St Martin-in-the-Fields

St Martins College of Art and Design. *See* Central St Martins

St Neot, Cornwall, but **St Neots**, Cambridgeshire

St Paul's Cathedral

St Stephen's Green, Dublin (not Stephen's Green)

St Thomas' Hospital, London

Saint-Saëns, the composer

saleroom (one word)

Salonika, rather than Thessaloniki. *See* foreign place names

salutary (not salutory)

Salvadorean (not -ian)

Sam-7 missiles

Sanaa, capital of Yemen (not Sana'a, Sana etc)

sanatorium, **sanatoriums** (plural) (not *sanitorium*)

sandpit (one word)

SANE, the schizophrenia charity, wishes to be known thus, caps rather than normal style of u/lc

Santer, Jacques, former President of the European Commission, is from Luxembourg, so call him Mr, not M. *See* foreign appellations

sarin (as in nerve gas), l/c

sat is the past tense and the past participle of "to sit". Never write that somebody "was sat" in his car, her living room etc; write "was seated" or "was sitting"

Satan, **Satanism** (initial caps), but **satanic**

SATs (standard assessment tasks) have now been replaced by national tests, such as Key Stage 1 tests

Sauchiehall Street, Glasgow

Saudi must never be used as short form for the country, Saudi Arabia. Confine its use to the adjectival, eg, Saudi Royal Family

Savile Row, **Savile Club**. *See* London clubs

Savile, Jimmy; Sir James in formal context only

Saville Theatre

SBS Special Boat Service (not Squadron)

Sca Fell, **Scafell Pike** are two separate mountains in the Lake District. Scafell Pike, at 978m (3,209ft), is the highest in England

Scalextric (not Scalectrix)

Scandinavia (never Scandanavia)

Scarborough, North Yorkshire

Scardino, Dame Marjorie (she has dual British-US nationality)

scarify take care; its meaning is to cut into, to cut skin from; its colloquial meaning of to terrify should be avoided wherever possible

scars do not heal (even metaphorically); wounds heal, scars remain

Schadenfreude (cap, italic) means the malicious enjoyment of another's misfortunes; do not misuse

Schiphol airport, Amsterdam

schizophrenic never use as a term of abuse and avoid as a metaphor. *See* medical terms, SANE

Schleswig-Holstein

Schoenberg, Arnold

schools cap when full title is given (if in doubt, consult the *Independent Schools Year Book* or the state sector equivalent, the *Education Year Book*); nowadays use the classifications of independent, state, grant-maintained, comprehensive, grammar, secondary modern (rarely), etc, rather than public, private etc (except in historical context). *See* headmaster

schoolchildren (one word), schoolgirl, schoolboy, schooldays, schoolmaster, schoolmistress and schoolteacher (rarely); but school-leaver

School Curriculum and Assessment Authority no longer exists; it has been replaced by the Qualifications and Curriculum Authority (QCA)

Schwarzenegger, Arnold

Schweitzer, Albert

scientific measures write out first time with abbreviations in parentheses, shorten thereafter. The abbreviation takes no point and no "s" in the plural, eg, 14km, not 14kms. Some basic international units and their abbreviations are: metre (m); gram (g); litre (l); ampere (A); volt (V); watt (W); note also kilowatt-hour (kWh).

Only abbreviate mile to *m* in mph and mpg; and gallon to *g* in mpg (otherwise gal). Beware of using *m* for million or for miles in any scientific context when it might be taken for metres. *See* metric, weights

scientific names when employing the Latin terminology, we must use the internationally accepted convention of initial cap on the first (generic) word, then l/c for the second (specific); eg, Homo sapiens, *Branta canadensis* (Canada goose) etc. For all but the most common we should also italicise

Scilly, Isles of do not use Scilly Isles; note spelling of St Mary's and Tresco

Scope is the new name for the former Spastics Society

Scotch, the whisky – not to be used as a substitute for the adjectives Scottish and Scots. But note Scotch broth, Scotch mist, Scotch egg and Scotch terrier; also note Scots pine

Scottish National Party (SNP) now cap Nationalists in the Scottish party context, but l/c nationalists in the wider sense

Scottish place names never say, eg, Motherwell, Scotland; instead say Motherwell, North Lanarkshire. Take care with new names under local government reorganisation; regions such as Central, Grampian and Strathclyde should now be referred to only in their historical context or if they persist in official titles such as Strathclyde Police or the University of Strathclyde. Permissible too to refer informally to the Central belt (between Edinburgh and Glasgow).

The same principle about counties applies to Wales and Northern

Ireland; give the county unless the town or city is big enough or well-enough known for the county to be unnecessary

Scottish Parliament cap "P". Note First Minister (not Secretary)

ScottishPower

Scott Thomas, Kristin (no hyphen)

Scouts no longer called Boy Scouts. *See* Guides

Scrabble (initial cap)

scrapheap (one word)

scratchcard (one word), as **smartcard**, **swipecard**

Scripture(s) cap as in Holy Scripture, but scriptural (l/c). *See* Christian terms

scriptwriter

sculptures in italic. With photographs of sculptures always give the sculptor's name. *See* Arts special section (page 18)

seabed, **seabird**, **seahorse**, **seagull**, **seasick** (no hyphens)

seasonal, but **unseasonable** (not unseasonal). Note also **seasonal affective disorder** (l/c), abbreviated to SAD

seasons always l/c when unattached, ie, spring, summer, autumn, winter; but Winter Olympics etc. Note also **summertime**, **wintertime**,

springtime, but **British Summer Time** (BST), and **Greenwich Mean Time** (GMT). *See* times

seatbelt

second-hand (hyphenated)

Second World War, not World War II/Two etc

Secret Intelligence Service (SIS, or MI6) takes caps. *See* Security Service (MI5)

Secret Service in the US protects the President and Vice-President. As a colloquial phrase in the UK it **must** be l/c, but prefer (to avoid confusion) to use Secret Intelligence Service (MI6 or SIS)

Secretary-General of the United Nations, Nato

Securities and Exchange Commission, the US regulator; do not use &. Write SEC after first mention

Securities and Investments Board (SIB), replaced in October 1997 by the Financial Services Authority (FSA)

Security Service (MI5) takes caps; but l/c for the security services in non-specific use. *See* Secret Intelligence Service

see-saw (hyphenate)

seize (never sieze)

select committees and parliamentary committees capped at first mention, or when full title is given, eg, the Foreign Affairs Select Committee; thereafter, the select committee, or the committee. *See* Politics special section (page 131)

Selfridges

sell-off, **sell-out** (but *see* buyout)

Sellotape is a trade name; otherwise, use *sticky tape* or *adhesive tape*

semiconductor

Semtex (cap)

Senate (US); Senator Edward Kennedy, then the senator; alternatively, Mr Kennedy, the Massachusetts senator

senior abbreviate to Sr (not Snr) in the American context, eg, Henry Ramstein Sr; *see* junior. Avoid the cliché *senior executive* when you mean *executive* – nine times out of ten the adjective is redundant (as *major*)

Senior Salaries Review Body (caps) has replaced the Top Salaries Review Body

septic tanks (never sceptic)

septuagenarian

Serb for the people but **Serbian** can be used (sparingly) as an adjective

Serious Fraud Office (SFO), but fraud squad. *See* Flying Squad

Serjeant at Arms

Serps spell out at first mention as state earnings related pension scheme (Serps)

serve in a warship (but *on* a merchant ship), and serve in (not on) a submarine, even though subs are boats, not ships. Important to make this distinction; readers complain every time we get it wrong. *See* Armed Forces special section (page 14)

Services, the (cap); or the Armed Services or the Armed Forces; also cap Service when used adjectivally as in *a Service family* (where meaning might otherwise be ambiguous); but l/c serviceman, servicewoman

Session, Court of, the supreme Scottish court (not Sessions). *See* Courts special section (page 47)

setback (noun); but to *set back*

sett, as with badgers

set-up try to find a synonym such as arrangement, organisation, structure, system etc

sewage is the waste matter; **sewerage** for the disposal system

sexism always be aware of sensitivities and be careful to avoid giving offence to women. It is often difficult to draw the line between sexism and political correctness

sex offenders register (l/c, no apostrophe)

Shadow cap in all cases, such as Shadow Cabinet, Shadow Environment Secretary, Shadow Chief Whip, a Shadow spokesman. *See* Politics special section (page 131)

Shah, Eddy (not Eddie)

shake-out, **shake-up** (but *see* buyout)

Shakespearean (not –ian)

shall, **should** keep up the vigorous defence of these against the encroaching *will* and *would*. Good practice is that *shall* and *should* go with the first person singular and plural (I shall, we shall), *will* and *would* with the others (he will, they will). *Shall* with second and third persons singular and plural has a slightly more emphatic meaning than *will*

shambles take care not to overwork this strong word, which means a slaughterhouse and, by extension, a scene of carnage

Shankill Road, Belfast (not Shankhill). *See* Ireland

shanks's pony (l/c)

Shangri-La

shantytown (one word)

SHAPE, Supreme Headquarters, Allied Powers, Europe (all caps)

share a joke banned in captions on photographs showing people laughing

share shop(s) (l/c)

Sharia means Islamic law; never use the tautology *Sharia law*

Sharm el-Sheikh, Egyptian resort in Sinai

sheikh (not shaikh)

shell suit (two words); but *see* tracksuit

Shepherds Bush

Sher, (Sir) Antony

Sherborne alumni of the Dorset public school are Shirburnians

sheriff (never sherrif)

Shetland or the Shetland Islands, not the Shetlands. *See* Orkney

Shia, not Shiite or any such variation; write Shia Muslims (as opposed to Sunni Muslims)

ships italicise the HMS when first mention of warship, eg, *HMS Sheffield*. Ships should generally be treated as feminine; thus *she* and *her* rather than *it* and *its*. *See* warships, boat, serve in

ships' tonnage for passenger ships, give gross tonnage in tonnes (rather than tons); cargo ships, deadweight tonnage. Check with *Lloyd's Register*

shock avoid in headlines unless in the electric context; in text, use the word as little as possible and never as a modifier, *shock revelations* etc (unless the context is ironic)

shock waves (two words), but use sparingly as a metaphor as it is becoming a cliché

shoo-in (not shoe-in), if you have to use this American phrase

shoot-out (hyphen), as in penalty shoot-out; but avoid in the sense of gunfight

shopkeeper, shopowner, shopfront, shoplift etc; but shop assistant and shop steward

shortlist (one word as noun or verb)

short-lived, short-sighted

showbusiness (one word); **showbiz** is an acceptable abbreviation in quotes and informal context

showcase avoid using as a verb. Use *display* or *exhibit* instead

showjumping one word except when it appears in a title such as the British Show Jumping Association, or is part of the name of an event that uses it as two words; similarly, **showjumper**

shrink, shrank (past tense), **shrunk** (or shrunken), past participle. *See* sink

Shroud of Turin (caps), or the Turin Shroud; subsequently, the shroud (l/c)

Siamese cats, twins; for Siam use Thailand except in historical context (adjective Thai)

Sichuan (not Szechuan, Setzuan, Szechwan or any other variant). *See* Chinese names

sickbed, as deathbed

side-effects

siege (never seige)

Siena only one "n"

sign language *not* deaf-and-dumb language

Silicon Valley, silicon chips, but **silicone implants** (for breasts etc)

silk barristers take silk and become silks (all l/c). *See* Courts special section (page 47)

Simon's Town, South Africa (not Simonstown). *See* South Africa

sin-bin (use hyphen)

Sindy doll (not Cindy)

singeing (from singe), to distinguish it from singing

sink, sank the past participle is **sunk**, the adjective **sunken**

siphon (not syphon)

Sistine Chapel (*not* Cistine)

sitcom (no hyphen) – permissible abbreviation for situation comedy

sit-in

situation avoid wherever possible; such phrases as *crisis situation, ongoing situation* and *no-win situation* are banned unless a direct quote positively demands them

Six Nations Championship
(rugby), no longer the Five Nations
Championship (England, Wales,
Scotland, Ireland, France and Italy).
See Sports special section (page 160)

sizeable

ski, skier, skied, skiing

skulduggery

Slavic must not be used; the noun
and adjective are **Slav**

slay is a biblical word, not to be
used in headlines for *kill* or *murder*

slimline (one word)

Slovak for the people and language,
Slovakian for the general adjective.
See Czech Republic, Croat, Croatian

smart aleck (not Alec)

smartcard (one word), as
scratchcard, swipecard

smelt (not smelled)

Smillie, Carol (not Smiley)

Smith, W H (no points). *See*
companies, initials

Smithsonian Institution, in
Washington (never Institute); can be
shortened to the Smithsonian

snarl-up do not use as a synonym
of *traffic jam*, *confusion* etc

sniffer dogs, **tracker dogs** avoid
these clichés wherever possible;
usually *dogs* is sufficient, but if the
context is unclear, say *police dogs*

snowball, **snowbound**, **snowdrift**,
snowfall, **snowman** etc

Soane's the museum in Lincoln's
Inn Fields is the Sir John Soane's
Museum

soap opera normally use rather
than just *soap*, though the latter may
have its place in less formal pieces, as
in the Diary or reviews

social chapter (l/c, as it is an
informal title)

**Social Democratic and Labour
Party** (the SDLP, in Northern
Ireland)

socialism, **socialist** for when to
cap, *see* communism, communist

soirée (use acute accent)

Solent, the (l/c the); but **The
Needles**

Solicitor-General (hyphen, as
Attorney-General); similarly
Solicitor-General for Scotland

Solicitors Complaints Bureau
(no apostrophes) has been replaced
by the **Office for the
Supervision of Solicitors**

Solti, Sir Georg (not George)

Solzhenitsyn, Aleksandr no
longer use Alexander. *See* Russian
names

sorcerer (not -or)

SOS

Sotheby's

soundbite

south, southeast, southern etc; for when to cap, *see* compass points

South, **Southern** (cap in US contexts)

South Africa never use the abbreviation SA, even in headlines.

The capital is Pretoria, which has the embassies (branches sometimes in Cape Town when Parliament is sitting) and government ministries. The legislature meets in Cape Town, and the Appeal Court sits in Bloemfontein. Pretoria can be referred to as the seat of government. Each of the new South African provinces has its own capital.

Say the **Eastern/Western/ Northern Cape** (caps); note also **KwaZulu/Natal** and **Simon's Town**.

Take care; several provinces have been renamed since the apartheid era, eg, **Mpumalanga** (formerly Eastern Transvaal); **Free State** (formerly Orange Free State); **Gauteng** (formerly Transvaal).

Say **southern Africa** when referring to Africa south of the Congo and Zambezi rivers

South Asia encompasses Afghanistan, Bangladesh, Bhutan, India, the Maldives, Nepal, Pakistan and Sri Lanka

South-East Asia comprises the ten Asean states – Indonesia, Singapore, Malaysia, Thailand, the Philippines, Brunei, Vietnam, Burma, Laos and Cambodia. Avoid calling Burma **Myanmar** (except occasionally in direct quotes). *See* Asean

South of France

Southern Ocean (caps)

southerner, l/c as **northerner**

Sovereign, the (cap). *See* monarch, Royal Family

Soviet Union *never* refer to *the Soviets* for the people or the Government, even in the historical context. The phrase is an Americanism often with disparaging overtones; a soviet is a committee, not a person. Refer instead to the *Soviet people* or *the Soviet Government* in historical context. *See* Russia, USSR

space avoid the phrase *outer space*. *See* Earth, Moon, Sun, Universe

Spanish regions use the Anglicised forms such as Andalusia (not Andalucía); Catalonia (not Cataluña), Navarre (not Navarra), Majorca (not Mallorca), Minorca (not Menorca) etc

spastic never use figuratively or as a term of abuse. *See* medical terms, Scope

Speaker always cap in parliamentary context

Speakers' Corner in Hyde Park (not Speaker's)

Special Branch (caps, but no *the*). *See* branch

special forces in the UK or US, generically l/c. But cap, eg, 5th Special Forces Group in US for specific units. *See* War on Terror

species both singular and plural in plant and animal sense. *See* scientific names

spellcheck, spellchecker (l/c, no hyphens) – but use with extreme care

spelt (not spelled); note misspelt

spiders are *not* insects, although like insects they are arthropods

Spielberg, Steven

spilt (not spilled)

spin, spun do not use *span* as past tense

spin-doctor (hyphen). *See* Politics special section (page 131)

Spiritualism, Spiritualist

split infinitives are banned, except in famous quotes such as "to boldly go where no man …" or in limited emphatic constructions such as "I want to live – to really live"

spoilt (not spoiled); but despoiled

spokesman, spokeswoman avoid where possible, eg, "the ministry said" rather than "a ministry spokesman said". *Official* is a useful alternative. Never use *spokesperson*. *See* chairman

sports clubs for when to use singular or plural, *see* teams

sportsmen, sportswomen omit the Mr, Mrs, Miss, Ms etc unless they are in news reports (eg, court hearings) in a specifically non-sporting context. *See* appellations

spots one word for **blackspot, hotspot, troublespot**, etc

sprang is the past tense of the verb to spring, eg, "she sprang into action"; **sprung** is the past participle, eg, "the wind has sprung up"

sprightly (*not* spritely)

spring-clean (hyphen)

squads in police context, usually l/c, but *see* Flying Squad; also note **Royal and Diplomatic Protection Squad**

Sri Lanka do not use Ceylon for the country except in historical context. But Ceylon tea etc

SSSI, site of special scientific interest (l/c)

Stability and Growth Pact (in the EU), can be shortened to the Stability Pact (keep caps)

stadium, plural stadiums. *See* referendum

Stalinist, Stalinism. *See* communism

stanch (verb), as "to stanch a flow of blood"; **staunch** is an adjective meaning loyal or firm

SPORTS

Sports writing is notoriously vulnerable to cliché and jargon. Apart from direct quotes, avoid the type of language used by players and television commentators.

GENERAL STYLE

- **All England Club**
- **baseball inning** (not innings)
- **Blue** (cap) from Oxford, Cambridge, for the award or the sportsman or woman
- **cross country** hyphenate only adjectivally, as in *cross-country trials*
- **Cup Final** the FA Cup Final, but l/c *final* for World Cup final, Worthington Cup final, and all other sporting cup finals (also FA Cup semi-final, l/c because by definition more than one)
- **divisions**, **groups**, **sections** etc in a sporting context always take l/c. Thus, World Cup group A, Nationwide League first division, European Championship section D etc
- **England Under-21** etc
- **first division**, **second division** etc (not Division One, 2, etc or any variant)
- **hat-trick** (cricket or football)
- **racecourse**, **racehorse**, but **horse race**, **horse racing**
- avoid **stretchered off**; say *carried off on a stretcher* instead
- **Super Bowl** (American football), two words
- refer to **women's** (not ladies') **competitions**, championships, events etc
- **World Cup** (caps), also **World Championship** (caps) in all sports

BOXING

- featherweight, heavyweight, light-heavyweight etc; knockout(s)

CRICKET

- wicketkeeper, mid-off, mid-wicket; follow on (verb) but the follow-on; hat-trick; hit-wicket; mis-hit; third man; extra cover; off break; leg-before; no-ball; a four (not 4); Norwich Union League; Cheltenham & Gloucester Trophy
- An off spinner is a bowler who bowls off breaks. Delivery in cricket is

a bowling action, not a ball: "Qadir has a puzzling delivery", not "Warne bowled Gatting with his first delivery"
- From January 1, 1997, the England and Wales Cricket Board (ECB) took control of all levels of the domestic game, and the Test and County Cricket Board (TCCB) is no more. The First-Class Forum (FCF) represents the views of the first-class counties. MCC (Marylebone Cricket Club) is concerned with the laws of cricket and matters at Lord's. Do not refer to **the** MCC

FOOTBALL

By itself, football means the association code. Soccer is an acceptable alternative

American football should always be described thus, unless the context is so obvious that football on its own is enough

- **General terms**: goalkeeper, kick-off (noun), Arsenal (not *the*), midfield, offside, play-off, shoot-out
- **Fifa** (not FIFA), football's governing body; similarly **Uefa** (not UEFA)
- **Champions League** (European football), no apostrophe; the later knockout stages of the competition (from quarter-final onwards) become the European Cup
- the **Football Association** (or **FA**), never the English Football Association
- St James' Park (both Newcastle and Exeter); St Andrew's, Birmingham (unlike St Andrews, golf)
- refer to the **Barclaycard Premiership** (no longer Carling) at first mention, the **Premiership** thereafter; the organisation that runs it is the **FA Premier League**. Take care not to confuse the competition and the organisation
- Similarly, the lower divisions form the **Nationwide League first division**, second division (note l/c) etc; this competition is run by the **Football League**

RUGBY UNION, RUGBY LEAGUE

Both rugby union and rugby league take l/c in general usage (though not, of course, in titles)

Never use the word rugger

Six Nations Championship, no longer Five Nations except in historical contexts

General terms: full back; scrum half; fly half; dropped goal; knock on (verb) but a knock-on (noun); scrummage; threequarter; open-side flanker; wing (not winger); lineout(s); 22-metre line, the 22; touch judge; triple crown; grand slam; the British Isles, not the British Lions (though Lions on its own is acceptable at second mention). NB: stand-off half in rugby league; **also replacements (not substitutes) in rugby union**

GOLF

The holes should appear in both text and results as 1st, 2nd, 10th, 18th, but write the "third extra hole" after that. In a matchplay use "Jones beat Brown 2 and 1" (not two and one). Usual *Times* style for numbers (spell out from one to ten, figures thereafter) in sentences such as "Faldo holed from eight feet/15ft"

General terms: the Open Championship (not British Open); bogey; birdie; eagle (no quotes); dormy, only if the match can be halved – a player cannot be dormy if the match can be taken to, say, the 19th hole to reach a decision; the Masters (not US Masters)

MOTOR RACING

- the British Grand Prix, Japanese Grand Prix etc (cap as specific); but grand prix racing etc (l/c, unspecific); plural grands prix
- Formula One motor racing (two caps, One spelt out)
- pitstop (one word)

SAILING

- sailing correspondent (not yachting correspondent)
- America's Cup
- Whitbread Round the World Race (caps, no hyphens)

SWIMMING

- freestyle, backstroke, breaststroke (no hyphens)

TENNIS

- Carlos Moyà (note accent)
- Flushing Meadows (not Meadow), New York, home of the US Open tennis championships

stand-off (noun, hyphen), but **standby** (noun, no hyphen)

Stansted airport (never Stanstead). *See* airports

stargazers, **stargazing**

Star Trek (two words, italic)

Start I, II, III etc (not Start 1, 2, 3), strategic arms reduction talks

State cap (sparingly) in context of the State as a wide concept, but not in the welfare state, or used adjectivally such as state benefits

stationary (not moving), **stationery** (writing materials)

Stationery Office, The (TSO abbreviated); no longer HMSO

stations l/c in Euston station, Waterloo station, Birmingham New Street station, but where possible, simply Euston, Waterloo etc. *See* airports

statistic(s) do not use as a fancy word for *figure(s)* or *number(s)*. Note that the Central Statistical Office has been replaced by the **Office for National Statistics** (not *of*). *See* National Statistics

status quo in roman, but the less familiar *status quo ante* in italics

statute book

stay home avoid this Americanism; say "stay at home"

Stealth bomber

Steel, Sir David the Presiding Officer (initial caps) of the Scottish Parliament prefers to be known as Sir David Steel in this context. In other contexts, continue to call him Lord Steel of Aikwood (first mention), Lord Steel thereafter

steelworks, **steelworker** etc

stepfather, **stepmother**, **stepson**, **stepdaughter**, but **step-family**, **step-parents**

Stephenson, George (trains), **Robert** (bridges); **Stevenson, Robert Louis, Adlai**

Stetson (initial cap)

still avoid writing the tautologous "still continues", "still remains" etc

Stilton (initial cap)

Stock Exchange caps for London and the New York Stock Exchange, l/c for all others; note l/c for the **stock market**

stony (not stoney)

storey (of a building); plural storeys

storm clouds two words, but try to avoid cliché of "gathering storm clouds"

storyteller, **storytelling**

straight be sparing in the use of this word to mean heterosexual. *See* gay

straight-faced, but **straightforward**

straitjacket

strait-laced; in **dire straits**

Strait of Hormuz (not Straits), **Strait of Gibraltar**, **Strait of Dover**

Stratford-upon-Avon except in the parliamentary constituency, which is Stratford-on-Avon

stratum plural strata

Streisand, Barbra

stress prefer *emphasise* as in "he emphasised the importance"

stricture means adverse criticism or censure, not constraint. Take care

strippagram

stylebook one word, as with guidebook, textbook etc (but **style guide**)

sub- like *multi-*, the hyphen here is often a question of what looks better. A random sample gives us **subdivision**, **sublet**, **subnormal**, **subsection**, **substandard**, **subtext**, **subcontract(or)**; in contrast, **sub-committee**, **sub-editor**, **sub-postmaster**, **sub-post office** etc. *See* hyphens, multi-

Subbuteo

sub-continent, the (l/c) for India, Pakistan and Bangladesh

subjects, academic use l/c for most subjects studied at school or university, eg, "she was reading

modern history with philosophy"; but where a proper name is involved, the cap is retained, eg, "he got a first in English literature and German after he dropped Latin in his second year"; and always cap Classics and PPE (short for philosophy, politics and economics). But note, eg, Professor of History when the phrase accompanies a name. *See* Professor, university posts

sub-let (as in property)

sub-machinegun. *See* machinegun

submarine always a boat, not a ship; *see* boat, ships, serve in

subplot, **subtext**, **subtitle**

subpoena, subpoenas, subpoenaing, subpoenaed

sub-Saharan Africa

subsequently prefer *afterwards* or *later*, and never say *subsequent to* when the meaning is *after*

subtropical (one word). *See* Tropics

such as do not confuse with *like*. *See* like

Sudan not the Sudan (except occasionally in historical context)

suing (not sueing), from *to sue*

summit avoid calling every high-level meeting a summit. Restrict its use to meetings of heads of government

summon the verb is to summon, the noun a summons (plural summonses). A person is summoned to appear before a tribunal etc; but a person in receipt of a specific summons can be said to have been summonsed

Sun. *See* Earth, Moon and Universe

sunbathing, **sunburn**, **sunglasses**, **suntan** etc but **sun-care** (products etc)

Super Bowl (as in American football)

superhighway (as in information superhighway); similarly, **superconductor**

superlatives beware of calling any person, event or thing *the first*, *the biggest*, *the best* etc without firm evidence that this is correct. Also, never say *first-ever*, *best-ever* etc. *See* ever, first, universal claims

supersede (never supercede)

superjumbo (one word), the new Airbus Industrie A3XX

supersonic (of speeds); for waves use ultrasonic

supervisor (*not* superviser)

supine means lying face-up. *See* prone

Supreme Court (US)

Surinam (not Suriname)

surprising (not suprising)

suspenseful do not use this abomination

Sussex always specify whether a place is in **East Sussex** or **West Sussex**, two separate counties

swansong (one word)

swap (not swop) do not use unless a mutual exchange is involved and never for organ transplants

swaths, not swathes (as in "cutting swaths through"); **swathes** to be used only as bandages

swatting (flies), **swotting** (study)

swearword (not hyphenated)

swingeing (as in cuts), to distinguish it from *swinging*

Swinging London, **Swinging Sixties** (caps)

swipecard, as scratchcard, smartcard

Symphony Hall, Birmingham, does not take "the". *See* Arts special section (page 18)

sync prefer to synch, as in the phrase "out of sync"

synod l/c on its own, but General Synod (caps). *See* Churches special section (page 37)

synthesizer (musical), but **synthesise** (chemical etc)

T

-t in nearly all cases, where there is a choice of past tense between a final -*t* or -*ed*, use -*t*, as in *burnt*, *spelt* etc. But NEVER *earnt*

tad heavily overworked as synonym of a little or a bit; avoid

tailback

Tajikistan

takeaway (meals)

take-off (aircraft)

takeover (noun), but *to take over* (verb)

takeover code but **Takeover Panel**

Taki Theodoracopulos, journalist and historian (Taki alone is acceptable after first mention)

Taleban now refer to **the** Taleban (or the Taleban authorities etc), and prefer the plural verb ("are" rather than "is" etc). *See* War on Terror

talk show, as chat show, game show, quiz show etc

talkSPORT, the radio station

Tallinn, Estonia

Tangier no final "s"

Tannoy is a trade name; use *loudspeaker* as alternative

Taoiseach (always cap). *See* Ireland

taramasalata (not taramo-). *See* hoummos

target beware lazy use of this word as a verb; eg, a campaign is *aimed at* or *directed at* children (rather than targeting children). Try to restrict its use to military (hostile acts) contexts. Note **targeted** (not targetted)

Tarmac is a trade name, but confine the cap version to the civil engineering company. Common usage allows the road surface or airport runway to be written as tarmac; **tarmacadam** is not a trade name

Tartars prefer to Tatars

task force (as in Falklands)

Tate Gallery the original gallery on Millbank is now known as Tate Britain, and the new one on Bankside as Tate Modern. Tate Liverpool and Tate St Ives retain their names

tattoos, tattooed, tattooing

taxman one word as colloquialism for Inland Revenue; similarly, no hyphen in **taxpayer**

Tchaikovsky

tea bag (two words), but **teacup**

teams normally plural, eg, "Manchester United were disappointing when they lost to Barcelona". But sports clubs usually take the singular, especially in news stories, eg, "Manchester City Football Club was fined heavily for crowd disturbances". There is some room for variation in this format, but whatever is decided, never mix singular and plural in the same story. Note hyphen in **team-mates**. *See* Sports special section (page 160)

teargas

Tea Room cap in the Commons Tea Room, but in general usage, one word and l/c, **tearoom**; similarly, **teashop**. *See* Politics special section (page 131)

Technicolor is a trade name. It must not be used except in that company's context. Use *multicoloured* as the general alternative

technology, media and telecoms companies/sector: abbreviate to TMTs

Tecs (initial cap only), short for training and enterprise councils. *See* Lecs

techMARK, the technology index

Teddy boy

Teesside (no hyphen, double "s" in middle); but note **Deeside** in both Scotland and Wales

teetotal

Tehran (not Teheran)

telephone numbers with three groups of figures, hyphenate only the first two (eg, 0151-234 8464). With new revised codes write, eg, 020-7782 5000, *not* 0207-782 5000

Teletext replaced Oracle (at the end of 1992) as the text service for ITV and Channel 4; do not use Oracle any more

Teletubbies (not Tellytubbies): Tinky Winky, Dipsy, Laa-Laa, Po. Singular is Teletubby

television TV is acceptable both in headlines and text. ITN (Independent Television News) is acceptable in its abbreviated form (in the same way as BBC). Write BBC Television, BBC One, BBC Two etc; but Argentine television, Norwegian television, etc (l/c unless we know it is the station's specific name). *See* BBC, ITV1, Channel 4, Radio 1

television and radio programmes are italicised. *See* Arts special section (page 18)

telltale (one word)

temazepam is a non-proprietary sedative, so l/c

temperatures the style is 16C (61F). Do not refer to temperatures as hot or cold; they are high or low. *See* celsius, metric

ten-minute rule (Bill) etc. *See* Politics special section (page 131)

Tennessee

tenpin bowling

Teresa. *See* Mother Teresa

Terminal 1, Heathrow (and Terminal 2, 3, 4, 5 etc). *See* airports, Heathrow

term-time (hyphenate)

Terre'Blanche, Eugene

Terrence Higgins Trust (not Terence)

Territorial Army, the Territorials (cap)

terrorist take care with this word and the associated *terrorism*; *guerrilla* is a less loaded word in the context of violent political struggle. Never use as a synonym of any dissident group that uses violence, eg, hunt saboteurs, and always try to specify groups as paramilitaries, gangster organisations or whatever. Remember, one man's terrorist is another man's freedom fighter

Tessa, tax-exempt special savings account

Test match should apply only to cricket (not rugby); for other sports, use the term international (match). *See* Sports special section (page 160)

textbook one word, as guidebook, stylebook, rulebook etc

TGV, *train à grande vitesse* (not *de*), the French high-speed train

thalidomide (l/c)

Thames Barrier, Thames Estuary (caps). *See* rivers

Thamesmead (near Erith), Thamesdown (Wiltshire administrative district), but Thames-side

that do not be shy of this word after *said, denied, claimed* etc; eg, "he denied that the evidence was confusing" is more elegant than "he denied the evidence was confusing". *That* is almost always better than *which* in a defining clause, eg, "the train that I take stops at Slough". As a general rule, use *which* for descriptive clauses and place it between commas, eg, "the night train, which used to carry newspapers, stops at Crewe". *See* ensure

Thatcher first mention Baroness Thatcher, thereafter Lady Thatcher. In historical context, preferable to say Mrs Thatcher or Margaret Thatcher, eg, "Mrs Thatcher took quick action in sending the task force to the Falklands". It would be wrong to say that her party forced Lady Thatcher from office in 1990. Note **Sir Denis** Thatcher (not Dennis)

theatre always attach Theatre (cap) to names at first mention, eg, the Criterion Theatre (thereafter the Criterion or simply the theatre). Some of the main London exceptions are the Old Vic, Young Vic, Palladium, Coliseum, Apollo Victoria, Donmar Warehouse, Hackney Empire; and outside

London, many such as the
Birmingham Hippodrome, Oxford
Playhouse, West Yorkshire Playhouse
etc. *See* Arts special section (page 18)

theatregoer

the then avoid expressions such as
"the then Prime Minister" or (worse)
"the then Mr Callaghan"; say "then
Prime Minister", "who was Prime
Minister at the time" or "Lord
Callaghan of Cardiff (then Mr
Callaghan)"

The Times almost always use italics
for the name of the newspaper,
except in headlines. But Times
Newspapers Ltd (roman), publisher
of *The Times* and *The Sunday Times*, is
the operating company of Times
Newspapers Holdings.

Also (in features headlines, etc)
The Times Gardener etc is an
acceptable style to avoid a mass of
italics and apostrophes.

In text, in the difficult area of
correspondents' and executive titles,
it is permissible to say "the *Times*
political correspondent", "the *Times*
wine correspondent" etc, although
"political editor of *The Times*", "wine
correspondent of *The Times*" etc are
preferable.

Always say "Editor of *The Times*",
"deputy editor of *The Times*" etc.

It is permissible to say "a *Times*
reader", "*Times* readers", but prefer
"readers of *The Times*". Similarly,
adjectival uses such as "a *Times* article",
"a *Times* offer" are acceptable.

Also note Times Law Report
(without The), but *The Times*
Crossword etc. Again, some
flexibility – to avoid a proliferation
of italics – can be used in puff
material etc.

For sections of the paper, avoid
italics: eg, T2 (no longer Times 2), *The
Times* Magazine, the Weekend section,
play, Crème, Law (supplement).

Keep phrases such as "told *The
Times*" to a minimum: *said* is usually
preferable.

Note supplements: *The Times
Educational Supplement*, *The Times
Higher Education Supplement*, *The
Times Literary Supplement*, and
Nursery World.

See correspondents, editor,
exclusive, News International

thermonuclear

Thermos must take the initial cap;
it is a trade name that must *always* be
observed

they should always agree with the
subject. Avoid sentences such as "If
someone loves animals, they should
protect them". Say instead "If people
love animals, they should protect
them"

think-tanks take care in describing
their ideological persuasions; we
should call the Social Market
Foundation (SMF), Demos and
Politeia independent think-tanks; the
Centre for Policy Studies (CPS) and
the Institute of Economic Affairs
(IEA) free-market or right-wing

think-tanks; and the Institute for Public Policy Research (IPPR) a left-wing think-tank

Third Way (caps), new Labour's political stratagem

Third World (caps)

threshold

throne cap sparingly, only in terms of the institution, eg, "he deferred to the wisdom of the Throne"; in other contexts, as with the chair itself, use l/c, eg, "The Queen came to the throne in 1952"

thunderbolts are mythological and do not exist; lightning bolts and thunderclaps do exist and can also be used metaphorically

thus far avoid; prefer *so far*

Tiananmen Square, Beijing

"tiger" economies of South-East Asia and the Pacific; use quotes where possible for first mention, subsequently without quotes, and always l/c

time bomb, but **timescale**, **timeshare**. *See* bombs

times never write, eg, 6pm last night, 9am tomorrow morning; say 6 o'clock last night or (if the context allows) 6pm, or 9am tomorrow. *See* seasons

Tinseltown (as in Hollywood), one word

Tipp-Ex

titles the most common solecism is to write Lady Helen Brown etc when we should say simply Lady Brown. As a quick rule of thumb, **no wife of a baronet or knight takes her Christian name in her title unless she is the daughter of a duke, marquess or earl**.

Some titles include a place name, eg, Lord Callaghan of Cardiff, Lord Archer of Weston-super-Mare, while others do not. Follow *Who's Who*, where **those whose place name must be included appear in bold caps**.

Always check with *Debrett* or *Who's Who* if in the slightest doubt. *See* Titles special section (page 171)

titles of books, films, discs, programmes etc avoid initial caps for every word (eg, do not write *The Hound Of The Baskervilles*). As a rule of thumb, use l/c for prepositions, conjunctions, definite and indefinite articles

toilet write lavatory wherever appropriate

together with avoid; prefer simply *with*; also beware such tautology as *blend together, meet together, link together* etc

Tolkien, J. R. R. (not Tolkein)

tomatoes (plural, as potatoes)

Tomlinson, Mike (prefer to Michael), former Chief Inspector of Schools

TITLES

ROYAL FAMILY

the Queen not usually necessary to write Her Majesty or HM the Queen, though occasionally Her Majesty can be used

Queen Elizabeth the Queen Mother (no commas); at first mention now write **the late Queen Elizabeth the Queen Mother**, thereafter the Queen Mother

the Duke of Edinburgh, thereafter the Duke or (sparingly) Prince Philip

the Prince of Wales, thereafter the Prince or (sparingly) Prince Charles

the Duke of York, thereafter Prince Andrew or the Duke

the Earl of Wessex, thereafter the Earl or Prince Edward; similarly, the Countess of Wessex, the Countess, or the former Sophie Rhys-Jones

the Princess Royal, thereafter the Princess; "Princess Anne" is no longer acceptable except in historical context

Commodore Tim Laurence, the Princess Royal's husband. No longer Captain

Diana, Princess of Wales, at first mention, thereafter the Princess (cap). The late Princess wherever appropriate. Never refer to Princess Diana or (even worse) Princess Di or Lady Di

Note also that **the Duchess of York** is no longer a member of the Royal Family since her divorce. After her first mention as Duchess of York, refer to the duchess (l/c) subsequently – never "Fergie" or any such vulgarity. Neither should she be called Sarah, Duchess of York

Royal Dukes keep the cap at subsequent mentions (eg, the Duke of Kent, later the Duke); other dukes do not retain the cap (see below)

PEERAGE AND KNIGHTS

Titles of nobility in descending order are as follows: **duke**, **marquess** (not marquis, except in foreign contexts and occasional Scottish titles), **earl**, **viscount** and **baron**. At first mention, give the formal title (as in *Who's Who*) eg, the Marquess of Paddington, the Earl of Waterloo, but then Lord Paddington, Lord Waterloo etc. This does not apply to **barons**, who are always **Lord** except in the announcement of new baronies. **Dukes** are always dukes and do not become Lord (eg, the Duke of Rutland). Note style of **the 2nd Earl, the 3rd Viscount** etc.

Baronesses in their own right or life peeresses are Baroness at first mention, and then Lady (eg, Baroness Thatcher, then Lady Thatcher).

The wife of a duke is a **duchess** (and is always called Duchess, eg, the Duchess of X); the wife of a marquess is a **marchioness**, of an earl a **countess**, of a viscount a **viscountess**. Use Lady at second and subsequent mentions. The **wife of a baronet**, eg, Sir John Euston, should be called **Lady** Euston from the start. Widows or former wives of all these titles who have not remarried use their Christian name before the title, eg, Margaret Duchess of Argyll (no commas). A widow may also be known as the Dowager Duchess of Y, or the Dowager Lady Z.

Apart from royalty (eg, the Duke of York), all these titles take l/c rather than cap after the first mention (eg, the Duke of Argyll, thereafter the duke).

Some titles include a place name, eg, Lord Callaghan of Cardiff, Lord Archer of Weston-super-Mare, while others do not. Again, **follow** *Who's Who*, **where those whose place name must be included appear in bold caps**.

Always give the full title at first mention, thereafter the abbreviated form, eg, Lord Bingham of Cornhill, thereafter Lord Bingham. Among titles spelt differently from the place name are the Marquess of Ailesbury, Marquess of Donegall, Earl of Guilford, Earl of Scarbrough.

Take great care with the use of **first names with titles**, especially the **wives** of peers, baronets and knights. The wife of Lord St Pancras is simply Lady St Pancras. The wife of Sir John Fenchurch is simply Lady Fenchurch (together, Sir John and Lady Fenchurch). However, when the name is a common one and there is no other convenient identification, or where there is some other compelling reason to give the first name, it is permissible to say Lady (John) Brown (brackets essential; see last sentence of next paragraph).

Baronets and **knights** are known as Sir John Smith, thereafter Sir John. Again, to repeat this essential point, **no wife of a baronet or knight takes her Christian name in her title unless she is the daughter of a duke, a marquess or an earl.** If a baronet has had more than one wife, the first wife is, eg, Mary Lady Smith (no commas) – the same form applies to the widow of a baron. If a knight has had more than one wife, the former wife puts her Christian name in brackets, eg, Lady (Alice) Brown, to distinguish her from the present wife, Lady Brown.

Also, if there are two baronets or knights with the same name, their wives (when mentioned apart from their husbands), put **his** Christian name in brackets, eg, Lady (Stephen) Brown, Lady (Andrew) Brown.

Dames of an order of chivalry take the same style as knights, eg, Dame Felicity Brown, thereafter Dame Felicity. A dame who is married may prefer to use her own style, eg, Dame Jennifer Jenkins, wife of Lord Jenkins of Hillhead; personal preferences should be respected.

CHILDREN OF PEERS

Eldest sons of a duke, marquess or earl use the father's second title as a courtesy title (eg, the Duke of Bedford's son is the Marquess of Tavistock). These people are not peers, even in headlines. **Younger sons** of dukes and marquesses use their first names and the family surname (eg, Lord John Worthington; subsequent mention, Lord John, never Lord Worthington; his wife is Lady John Worthington).

A woman is Lady Olive York etc only if she is the **daughter** of a duke, marquess or earl; in subsequent mentions, she is Lady Olive, never Lady York. Younger sons of earls and all children of viscounts and barons have the style the Hon, but it is unnecessary to use this except in Court Page copy; normally, they are simply Mr, Miss, Ms etc (none is a peer).

ANNOUNCEMENT OF TITLES

Baronets, knights and dames take the appropriate title as soon as the honour is announced. Peers have to submit their choice of title for approval, so wait until the formal public announcement (usually in *The London Gazette*).

tons, tonnes prefer to use *tonnes* in most contexts, though in historical passages tons would be more appropriate

Tontons Macoute (in Haiti); plural, no final "s"

Top Salaries Review Body is now called the Senior Salaries Review Body

Top Ten, Top 20, Top 40 etc (in musical or other lists)

tornado, plural **tornados** (storms); also Tornado, Tornados (aircraft)

torpedo, but plural **torpedoes**

Torvill (**Jayne**) and **Dean** (**Christopher**)

Tory, Tories acceptable alternative for Conservative(s). Do not write Tory Party with cap "P", but Tory party is permissible. *See* Conservative, committee (for 1922 Committee), select committees, and Politics special section (page 131)

totalisator, tote take l/c, no quotes; the Tote refers to the organisation

touchpaper

towards (not toward)

townhouse (one word)

Toys 'R' Us

tracker dogs, sniffer dogs avoid these clichés wherever possible; usually *dogs* is sufficient, but if the context is unclear, say *police dogs*

tracksuit (one word), but shell suit

Trade Descriptions Act

trade-in (noun or adjective), but *to trade in*

trademark (one word)

trade names many names of products in common use are proprietary and must be given a capital letter (at risk of legal action if we fail to do so); eg, **Biro, CinemaScope, Dictaphone, Hoover, Jeep, Kodak, Land Rover, Lycra, Perspex, Polaroid, Rollerblade, Tannoy, Technicolor, Thermos, Walkman, Xerox, Yale lock**. Be especially careful about drugs; try to use non-proprietary words such as aspirin, sleeping pills etc

trade unions (plural), not trades unions; but Trades Union Congress. *See* TUC

train companies South West Trains (no hyphens); ScotRail; Virgin CrossCountry; c2c (the Southend line); WAGN (no need to spell out West Anglia Great Northern); South Central (no longer Connex South Central); First Great Western; First Great Eastern etc

trainspotter, trainspotting (no hyphens)

tranquilliser, tranquillity

transatlantic, transcontinental; but **cross-Channel**

transistor do not use on its own in sense of transistor radio

Transit Van (initial caps, proprietary)

transpire means to come to light or to leak out. Do not use as an alternative of to happen or occur

Transport for London (abbreviate TfL) has replaced London Transport. Do not write Transport in London

transsexual (no hyphen); but **trans-ship**

Trans-Siberian Railway

Transvaal, but a Transvaler. *See* South Africa

trauma, traumatic avoid in the clichéd sense of *deeply upsetting, distressing* etc; it should be confined to its medical meaning of severe shock after an accident or stressful event

travellers, New Age travellers. *See* Gypsy, hippy

traveller's cheques

Travellers Club (no apostrophe). *See* London clubs

Triads (cap) in Chinese gangster context

Tricolour cap for the French flag, l/c in more general context

trillion American for a thousand billion (or a million million, 1,000,000,000,000), and should be explained as such in stories about overseas budgets, for example. Try to avoid in stories about Britain

Trinity College Dublin (no comma)

triple crown in rugby. *See* Sports special section (page 160)

tripos (l/c general context), but the History Tripos etc

trolleys (plural of trolley, not –ies)

Trooping the Colour (not of the Colour); also, **beating retreat**

Tropics, the (cap); note also the **Tropic of Capricorn/Cancer**, but **tropical, subtropical** l/c

Troubles, the. *See* Ireland

troubleshooter (one word); also **troublespot**

truck permissible in certain contexts. *See* lorry

Truman, Harry S. (former US President), but **Trueman, Fred**, cricketer

try to the verb *try* must be followed by *to* before the next verb, never by *and*, eg, "I will try to cross the road", not "I will try and cross the road"

Tsar (not czar), Tsarevich, Tsaritsa (not czarina); caps with the name, l/c in general sense. But note exceptions for government-appointed co-ordinators such as drugs czar, mental health czar

TSB formerly the Trustee Savings Bank, now part of Lloyds TSB

T-shirt

Tube (cap) acceptable in context on its own for the London Tube, or London Underground. Also cap the various lines such as Central Line, Metropolitan Line, Victoria Line etc

tuberculosis the adjective is *tuberculous*, not *tubercular*

TUC the Trades Union Congress. Note, first mention, General Council of the TUC, thereafter general council. General Secretary of the TUC should be capped (as leader of the national body), but general secretaries of individual unions retain the l/c

tug-of-war

tunku (Malaysian prince); cap before name, otherwise l/c. *See* Malaysia

turbo-jet, **turbo-prop**. *See* aircraft

Turin Shroud (caps), then the shroud (l/c)

Turkey parties take the cap, as in Motherland Party, Welfare Party, True Path Party etc

turn down prefer *reject* or *refuse* (except of beds)

turnlines are in bold, set right on the front page (and on inside pages where the story begins and spills) – eg, **Continued on page 2, col 7** – and set left on inside pages, eg, **Continued from page 1**

turn-off, **turn-on** (nouns), but no hyphens in **turnout**, **turnaround**, **turnabout**

Tussaud's, Madame, but note the Tussauds Group (no apostrophe), which also includes the London Planetarium, Warwick Castle, Alton Towers and Chessington World of Adventures

Tutankhamun never permit a break as Tutan-khamun; if the name has to be broken on a turn, it may be hyphenated as Tut-ankhamun or Tutankh-amun

Tutsis. *See* Hutus

TV. *See* television

TV-am no longer exists

Twentieth Century Fox

twentysomething, **thirtysomething**, and **fortysomething** etc (if this modern cliché has to be used at all)

Twin Towers (of Wembley) (caps)

twin towers (of the former World Trade Centre); the **northern tower** and the **southern tower** (all l/c). *See* War on Terror

twofold, **threefold**, **fourfold**, **tenfold** etc

two minutes' silence (the). *See* Armistice, Remembrance

two thirds, **three quarters** etc, but a two-thirds share (hyphenate adjectival use). Such expressions usually take the plural verb, eg, "three quarters of the children prefer horror films"; the same applies even in "a third of the children prefer blancmange". But note "two thirds of the bus was empty"

Tyne and Wear (not &)

typify, **typified** etc (not typefy)

Tyrol (not Tirol)

U

U no full point after Burmese prefix, eg, U Nu

Ucas (not UCAS), abbreviation of Universities and Colleges Admissions Service

Uefa (not UEFA), Uefa Cup. *See* Cup, and Sports special section (page 160)

UK acceptable abbreviation for United Kingdom in both text and headlines. But be careful that it is strictly applicable. *See* Britain

Ukraine omit *the*

Ulster permissible, especially in headlines, but use Northern Ireland or the Province when possible. *See* Ireland

ultimate use sparingly. *Ultimate limit* means *limit*

ultimatums (not ultimata). *See* referendum

ultraviolet

UMIST, the University of Manchester Institute of Science and Technology (caps, rather than Umist)

unchristian (l/c). *See* Christian

uncoordinated (but co-ordinate). *See* hyphens

under-age (hyphenated, as **over-age**)

underestimate

Underground, London. *See* Tube

underreact

undervalue

underwater one word as adjective, eg, underwater exploration; but two words as adverb, eg, the couple were married under water

under way (*always* two words)

Unesco, the United Nations Educational, Scientific, and Cultural Organisation. *See* United Nations

UNHCR, the United Nations High Commissioner for Refugees. *See* United Nations, paragraph (d)

Union Jack, except in most naval and some ceremonial contexts, when **Union Flag** is correct; note that in the Royal Navy, Union Jack is used only when flown at the jackstaff

Unionist cap in Ulster political context. *See* Ireland

unique means only one, having no like or equal. Do not use except in this specific sense. Phrases such as *very unique, even more unique,* are thus nonsense and are banned

unitary authorities since the abolition of Avon, Humberside and Cleveland, plus wholesale reorganisation of Welsh and Scottish local government, we should take care how we locate towns in these areas.

Places in the **former county of Avon** should now be described as in either Gloucestershire or Somerset. **Hereford and Worcester** no longer exists as a unitary authority; it has been replaced by a new Worcestershire County Council and a new unitary authority for Herefordshire.

Berkshire County Council has been replaced by the unitary authorities of Bracknell Forest, Reading, Slough, Windsor and Maidenhead, and Wokingham. The area around Newbury, stretching east to Reading and west to the Wiltshire border, is now called **West Berkshire**.

Places in the **former Humberside** should be located as either East Riding (north of the Humber) or Lincolnshire (south of the river).

The scrapping of **Cleveland** and reorganisation of **Yorkshire** creates all kinds of difficulties. The simplest solution will be to locate places in either North Yorkshire (new authority, hence cap "N"), the East Riding (of Yorkshire) (also a new authority), or South or West Yorkshire. Although these latter two are not unitary authorities, they are still cohesive regions such as West Midlands or Greater Manchester; and note, West Yorkshire Police etc. If in doubt, say simply Yorkshire. Examples: Thirsk, North Yorkshire; Bridlington, East Riding; Rotherham, South Yorkshire; Keighley, West Yorkshire.

For **Wales**, note that Clwyd, Dyfed and Gwent no longer exist as authorities, so unless the new county has a traditional and generally familiar name (eg, Pembrokeshire, Carmarthenshire, Powys, Denbighshire etc), it will often be simpler to locate smaller towns and villages just as in North Wales, Mid Wales, West Wales, South Wales. Note that **Gwynedd** does still exist as a unitary authority, though smaller than when it was a county. If in doubt, use one of the North, Mid, West, or South designations.

For **Scotland**, regions such as Central, Grampian and Strathclyde should now be referred to only in their historical context or if they persist in official titles such as Strathclyde Police or the University of Strathclyde. Permissible too to refer informally to the Central belt (between Edinburgh and Glasgow), despite the scrapping of Central region

United Nations, or the UN; usually no need to spell out even at first mention. Other points:

a. Secretary-General of the UN (now Kofi Annan)

b. UN Security Council, UN General Assembly at first mention, and thereafter keep the caps, as in the Security Council, the General Assembly

c. UN derivatives such as Unesco, Unifil, Unprofor etc are written thus where the word can be voiced. *See* initials

d. The UN High Commissioner for Refugees (never Commission) is the organisation, as well as a person. Abbreviate to UNHCR after first mention

United Reformed Church (not Reform). *See* Churches special section (page 37)

United States (of America) is always followed by a singular verb. Common usage allows abbreviation to US in text as well as headlines, but do not ignore the word America. *See* America(n), New York, Washington

units Downing Street policy unit (l/c), but the Social Exclusion Unit (initial caps), as it has official status. *See* Downing Street

universal claims always beware of claiming that something is the first or last of its kind, or that someone is the first person to ... or the last surviving member of ... or the oldest inhabitant etc. *See* ever, first, superlatives

Universe cap in planetary context, as Sun, Earth, Moon etc, but l/c in

phrases such as "she became the centre of his universe"

universities always cap as in Birmingham University (or the University of Birmingham), Sussex University, the University of East Anglia etc; thereafter, the university l/c. If in doubt about the proper title, consult *The Times Good University Guide*. *See* Cambridge, Oxford, London, Vice-Chancellor

University College London (no comma; *see* London University); similarly, **University College Dublin**

university posts at first mention, cap Vice-Chancellor, Chancellor, Pro-Vice-Chancellor, Pro-Chancellor, Dean, Master, Professor, Fellow etc; at subsequent mentions, l/c; eg, Dr Mark Blodkin, Professor of Modern History at Kent University, said ... later, the professor said ...

unlikeable, unloveable

unmistakable (not one of those with the middle "e")

unparalleled

unshakeable

Untouchables (in Indian caste system), cap

unveil take care with this word, which means to remove a covering from something, or (by extension) to disclose. It should not be used in phrases such as unveiling a ship, or unveiling a flag

up avoid unnecessary use after verbs, as in meet up, rest up, end up. *See* down

upbeat, **upgrade**, **upfront**

upmarket, as downmarket

upon take care with use of *up, upon, up on*, and *on*; eg, "The cat jumped **on** the floor, **upon** the mouse, **up on** the table, then **up** the tree"

Upper House, **Lower House**. *See* Politics special section (page 131)

Uruguay Round (caps), the world trade deal. *See* Gatt, World Trade Organisation

US. *See* America(n), United States

USSR avoid wherever possible; say Soviet Union instead (and now only in historical context). *See* Russia

utilise almost always prefer *use*

Utopia, **Utopian** (cap)

U-turn is an overworked phrase, especially in the political context. Be sparing in its use, particularly when only a minor change of policy direction is involved

V

vacuum in common use as a verb, but avoid Hoover, a trade name. *See* Hoover, trade names

vagaries means aimless wanderings or eccentric ideas, not vicissitudes or changes (as in weather)

Vajpayee, Atal Behari (Indian politician)

Valentine's Day (normally omit the St), and keep cap for **Valentine card** etc

Valium (proprietary, so cap)

Valletta (Malta)

valley cap in full name, such as the Thames Valley, the Wye Valley etc. *See* Welsh Valleys

Van in Dutch names is cap when surname alone is given, as in **Van Gogh**, but l/c when used in full, eg, **Vincent van Gogh**. Note Ludwig van Beethoven (not von), although the composer was German. *See* von

Van Dyck, Sir Anthony, but vandyke brown, vandyke beard etc

Vanessa-Mae, the violinist (note hyphen)

Van Outen, Denise (cap "V")

various do not use as a pronoun as in "various of the countries protested"; write "several/many of the countries …"

Varsity match acceptable colloquialism for the Oxford–Cambridge rugby match

VAT, value-added tax; no need to spell out fully

V-chip (electronic scramblers for TV)

VE-Day. *See* D-Day, VJ-Day

Velázquez (Diego Rodríguez de Silva y Velázquez, but normally last name on its own will suffice), the 17th-century Spanish painter (not Velasquez)

Velcro (cap, proprietary)

veld, not veldt

ventricles (anatomical), not ventricals

veranda (no final "h")

verbal means pertaining to words, oral means pertaining to the mouth. Do not confuse. Sadly, corrupted phrases such as *verbal abuse* and *verbal warning* have permeated sports journalism to the point of our having to accept them occasionally, but always try to restrict such use and find an alternative. *See* oral

verbosity watch out for, and eliminate, wordy phrases such as "on the part of" (use *by*), "a large number of" (*many*), "numerous occasions" (*often*), "this day and age" (does not even demand an alternative). Such meaningless expressions have no place in *The Times*

verdict do not use for civil hearings – verdicts come at the end of criminal trials. *See* employment tribunals, industrial tribunals

verger, **virger** the latter to be used in context of St Paul's and Winchester Cathedrals

vermilion (not vermillion)

versus abbreviation is v (l/c, no point)

very one of the most overworked words in English. Always try to do without

vetoes (plural)

viable do not use as a synonym of feasible or practicable; it means capable of independent existence

vicar take care not to use as a generic word for priest, parson or clergyman. Vicar means specifically the incumbent of a parish (unless a rector); if in doubt, *clergyman* is usually a safer word. *See* Churches special section (page 37)

vice always hyphenate in its deputy context (vice-chairman, vice-president of a company etc) but not

in its depravity context, eg, vice squad. Do not confine the meaning of vice to sex; it is the opposite of virtue and has a correspondingly wide range of meaning

Vice-Chancellor of a university should be capped at first mention, then l/c. *See* university posts, job titles

vice versa (roman, no hyphen)

Victoria and Albert (Museum) use the ampersand only in the abbreviated **V&A**

videoconference, **videoconferencing** (no hyphen)

videotape (one word); but video cassette, video recorder/recording. A video (for the film recording) is now common usage and permissible

Vietcong (not Viet Cong)

vintage car is one made between 1919 and 1930; **veteran car** is one made before 1919

Virgil (not Vergil)

Virtuality is a trade name and must be capped; it must not be used as a synonym of virtual reality

viruses. *See* bacteria

vis-à-vis (roman, hyphens, with accent)

viscountcy describes the rank. *See* Titles special section (page 171)

vitamin A, **B**, **C** etc (l/c "v")

viz prefer *namely*, *that is*, or even *ie*

VJ-Day. *See* D-Day, VE-Day

vocal cords (not chords)

Vodafone (not Vodaphone)

voiceover (no hyphen)

volcanoes (plural of volcano)

volte-face (roman, hyphenated)

von (German) is usually l/c in the middle of a name, and capped only at the beginning of a sentence. *See* Van

Vosper Thornycroft (not Thorneycroft), and renamed **VT Group** (summer 2002)

VP never use as abbreviation of Vice-President of the US or other state (or vice-president of a company)

W

wacky (not whacky)

wagon

Wales cap North Wales, South Wales, Mid Wales, West Wales. For new counties under the local government reorganisation of 1996, *see* unitary authorities

walked free from court avoid this lazy cliché

Walkman is a trade name, so must cap; in general sense, use *personal stereo*

walkout

Wallace and Gromit (not Grommit)

Wall's (ice-cream etc)

Wal-Mart

Walton, Izaak, author of *The Compleat Angler*

Wap (as in mobile telephones), short for wireless application protocol (not WAP)

war crimes tribunal cap only when using the full title, **the International Criminal Tribunal for the Former Yugoslavia**. It sits at The Hague and has a President and a Chief Prosecutor

war game(s) (two words)

warfarin is not a trade name, so l/c

warn is a transitive verb that requires a direct personal object; in other words, a person has to warn somebody about something. Do not say "The Chancellor warned that taxes would rise"; say "The Chancellor **gave warning that/ issued a warning that ...**", or alternatively, "The Chancellor **warned MPs that ...**". So try always to find an object with the verb; eg, X warned the City that ..., Y warned voters that ..., rather than the somewhat cumbersome "gave warning" formula. However, we can afford some flexibility in headlines where, eg, *Teachers warn of school closures* would be acceptable

War on Terror if the caps on War on Terror look obtrusive or overused, adopt a l/c alternative such as war against terrorism. Frequently used names and terms arising from the terrorist attacks against the US on September 11, 2001, include: **Osama bin Laden**; **al-Qaeda** (his terrorist group); **al-Jazeera** (TV station in Qatar); **burka** (prefer to burqa); **Pashtuns** (biggest ethnic group in Afghanistan – they speak **Pashto**); **Loya Jirga** (Afghan national council that meets irregularly); **special forces** (l/c) of the US or UK in generic sense; **twin towers** (of the former World Trade Centre; note the **northern tower** and the **southern tower**, all l/c); **Ground Zero**; **King Zahir Shah** (returned Afghan King; King Zahir at subsequent mentions); **Mullah Muhammad Omar** (supreme leader of the Taleban; Mullah Omar at subsequent mentions). Note also **Camp X-Ray** at **Guantanamo Bay** (no accent), Cuba

wars cap the First World War, Second World War, Cold War, Korean War, the Vietnam War, the Six Day War (no hyphen), the Gulf War etc; but prefer the **Falklands conflict** because war was never formally declared; if the phrase has to be used, write Falklands war (l/c)

warships take care with the following distinction: to serve **in** a warship, but **on** a merchant ship; a naval officer is **appointed** to serve **in** HMS *Sheffield*, and not *posted* to serve. *See* Armed Forces special section (page 14)

wartime

Washington not usually necessary to add DC (as in Washington DC), but occasionally useful to distinguish it from Washington State (caps). That and New York State are the only two states we need to cap, to avoid confusion. *See* New York

washout (one word)

waste usually better to write *waste* than *wastage*, which means the process of loss, or its amount or rate

wastepaper bin/basket

watchdog

watercolour, **watercolourist**; but Royal Society of Painters in Water Colours

water lily (two words), but artistic convention uses one word in Monet's *Waterlilies* paintings

Waterstone's (with apostrophe), the booksellers

wear say menswear, women's wear, children's wear, sportswear. *See* clothing

weather stories (about floods, hurricanes, snow, record sunshine etc in the UK) must always take a cross-reference to the back page weather forecast. Style is, eg, **Forecast, page 24** (bold, set right), or **Weather Eye, page 24**

week, **weekend** the week ends on Saturday night. Common sense will dictate whether to say last week, this week, next week etc. Beware of references to *at the weekend* in Monday papers: always make clear whether you mean the weekend just past or next Saturday and Sunday. The phrase "this weekend" should refer only to the coming weekend

weigh anchor means to raise a vessel's anchor, not to drop it. *See*

Armed Forces special section (page 14) (Royal Navy)

weights and measures abbreviations context will determine when to shorten kilometres, grams, feet, inches, stones, pounds, ounces etc. "He was 6ft 7in" (not ins, and no space between number and abbreviation); but "she stood two feet from the kerb". Similarly, "she weighed 8st 12lb" (not lbs); but "he was several pounds overweight". *See* scientific measures, metric

Welch, Welsh take care with **The Royal Welch Fusiliers**, but **Welsh Guards** (part of The Guards Division). *See* Armed Forces special section (page 14)

welfare state (l/c); but note the **Welfare to Work** programme (twice cap W, no hyphens). *See* State

wellbeing

wellington boots (l/c)

wellwisher (do not hyphenate)

Welsh Assembly, caps, and the Assembly (cap) thereafter. The leader of the Assembly is called the **First Minister** (no longer the First Secretary)

Welsh Valleys for the (former) mining valleys of South Wales

Welsh, Irvine (the novelist and playwright)

west, western etc; for when to cap in geographical context, *see* compass points

West, the (in global political sense); similarly, **Western** leaders, Western Europe etc

Westbrook, Danniella

western (l/c for cowboy films)

West Lothian question (l/c "q"). *See* Politics special section (page 131)

whereabouts is singular, eg, "his whereabouts is not known". Prefer "nobody knows where he is"

whether rarely needs or *not* to follow it

which. *See* that

while (not whilst)

whingeing (with middle "e")

whips cap Chief Whip, Whips' Office, but l/c the unspecific, eg, a government whip. *See* Politics special section (page 131)

whisky (from Scotland), **Scotch** as alternative; but **whiskey** (from Ireland and America). *See* Scotch

whistle-blower

whistle-stop (tour etc)

Whitbread Round the World Race (note caps, no hyphens)

White Cliffs of Dover (caps)

white-collar workers

White Paper (caps), as with Green Paper; these should not be capped, however, with anything other than a White Paper/Green Paper issued by the Government. A "white paper" from the Opposition should be styled thus – quotes and l/c first mention, thereafter just l/c. *See* Green Paper, Politics special section (page 131)

whiz-kid only one "z", but use this colloquialism sparingly

WHO spell out at first mention, World Health Organisation, then the WHO

who, whom which of these to use is determined solely by its function in the relative clause. Remember that *whom* has to be the object of the verb in the relative clause. Thus, "she is the woman whom the police wish to interview" (ie, the police wish to interview *her*, not *she*); the other most common use of *whom* is after a preposition such as *by, with* or *from*, eg, "the person from whom he bought a ticket". Beware of traps, however: "Who do you think did it?" is correct (not *whom*, because who is the subject of "did it", not the object of "do you think"); and "Give it to whoever wants it" is correct (not *whomever*) because *whoever* is the subject of the verb wants. Beware too of constructions such as "he squirted ammonia at a van driver who [correct] he believed had cut him up" (where "he believed" is simply an interjection; "who" is not the object of "he

believed" but the subject of the subordinate clause, "who … had cut him up")

whodunnit (not whodunit)

Who Wants to be a Millionaire? (note caps, l/c and question mark)

why usually superfluous after *reason*, eg, "the reason he did it was …", not "the reason why he did it was …"

Wicks Committee on Standards in Public Life (Sir Nigel Wicks new chairman, March 2001). *See* Committee

Widdecombe, Ann (not Anne)

Widdicombe Fair (not Widdecombe); note Uncle Tom Cobbleigh

wide no hyphen in compounds such as **countrywide, nationwide, worldwide**

wideawake, always one word

widow (woman), **widower** (man); never say "widow of the late John Jones"; she is the "widow of John Jones"

wildfowl, wildlife

Wild West

Wimbledon caps for the Centre Court, No 1 Court, No 14 Court etc. *See* Sports special section (page 160)

Winchester College its pupils are Wykehamists

wind with strong winds, give a description as well as force number (in numerals), eg, storm force 10 (add "on the Beaufort scale" where appropriate. The scale grades wind speeds from 0 to 12; Americans use the scale to 17). So write, eg, force 4 (l/c, numeral), up to force 7; thereafter, gale force 8, severe gale force 9, storm force 10, violent storm force 11 and hurricane force 12. But the vernacular "force 11 winds" is acceptable

wind farm (two words)

wines l/c in most cases, for both the type and the grape, except where it would look out of place; so say, eg, bordeaux, burgundy, champagne, claret, moselle, alsace, rioja, but a Côtes du Rhône, a Hunter Valley chardonnay. Cap when referring specifically to the wine-growing region, eg, "I prefer a good burgundy to an alsace, but I think the best wines still come from Bordeaux"; "he preferred to buy his champagne only in Champagne"

wine bar (two words)

Winnie-the-Pooh has hyphens

Winslet, Kate

Winter of Discontent (of 1978–79), initial caps

Wirral (not Wirrall); permissible to refer to The Wirral (cap "T"), but the Wirral peninsula

wish list (no hyphen)

wistaria (not wisteria)

witch-hunt, but **witchcraft**

withhold (not withold)

witnesses in British courts witnesses go into the witness box and give evidence; they do not take the stand and testify. In the general sense, prefer *witness* to *eyewitness* wherever possible. *See* eyewitness

woebegone, woeful

Wolf Cubs are now Cub Scouts. *See* Boy Scouts

women doctors, women teachers etc adopt the plural through common usage. *See* feminine designations, lady

Woodgate, Jonathan (not Jonathon), footballer

Woolf reforms several important changes have been made in civil litigation rules and terminology since April 1999. Three of the commonest are: plaintiffs are now **claimants**; a writ is now a **claim form**; and **notices of application** will be served in the place of summonses. For fuller list, *see* Courts Special Section (page 47)

Woolsack (in Parliament), initial cap

Woolworths no apostrophe either in formal name for business contexts or colloquial use for the store and products

**word-processor,
word-processing** (hyphens)

workaholic, as shopaholic, but note chocoholic

**workers farmworkers,
metalworkers** and **roadworkers** each one word, but two for **car workers, oil workers, office workers** etc

**workforce, workshop,
work-to-rule**

working families tax credit (l/c, and families, not family)

workout (one word); also **workrate**

world avoid, wherever possible, phrases such as the fashion world, the theatre world, the cricket world etc

World Heritage Site (caps)

World Trade Organisation (WTO), the successor body to Gatt. *See* Gatt, Uruguay Round

World Wide Fund for Nature (WWF) (not Worldwide; nor World Wildlife Fund, its old name); the general adjective is **worldwide**. *See* WWF

world wide web (as with internet), l/c; and the **web** for short, also **website**. *See* internet

Worrall Thompson, Antony (TV cook)

worthwhile (one word) often used

where simply **worth** would be better, eg, "the programme was worth recording"

wrack means seaweed or wreckage and must not be used as a synonym of *torture*; thus, *racked by doubts* etc. *See* racked

wreaked (not *wrought*) havoc, heavy damage, vengeance etc

Wrens use only in historical context. Women sailors are now fully integrated into the Royal Navy and the WRNS no longer exists as a separate entity. If necessary to specify, refer to a woman captain etc

write-off (noun), **write-up** (noun), but a **writedown** (in business context)

writes with written-in bylines, prefer the construction *Ann Bloggs writes* to *writes Ann Bloggs*. Use the singular with, eg (Our Foreign Staff writes). Normal style is to use the brackets on news and sports pages, the italics on features

wrongdoer, wrongdoing, but **wrong-footed, wrong-headed**

WWF is the abbreviation of the World Wide Fund for Nature and for legal reasons must not be used for the World Wrestling Federation (say *the federation* if a shorter form for the wrestling group is needed). *See* World Wide Fund for Nature

Wyndham's Theatre in London takes the apostrophe

X

xenophobe, xenophobia

Xerox is a trade name, so must cap

Xhosa (not Khosa), plural Xhosas, the Bantu tribe

Xmas must *not* be used in *The Times* (unless part of special title or in a direct quote etc)

X-ray fully acceptable abbreviation of X-ray examination. It can also be used as a verb, to X-ray someone. Note, however, Camp X-Ray at Guantanamo Bay, Cuba. *See* War on Terror

Y

Yangtze (not Yangtse)

Yardies (West Indian criminal gangs)

Yarmouth is on the Isle of Wight; the town on the Norfolk coast is Great Yarmouth

Yellow Pages italics for the book, but roman for the organisation

Yemen (not *the* Yemen)

"yes" vote, "no" vote

yeti (l/c), the abominable snowman

YMCA, YWCA

yoghurt

yoke (oxen), **yolk** (egg); *never* confuse

Yorkshire since the reorganisation of 1996, *see* unitary authorities for how to locate places in the county. Specify the location for smaller towns and villages, eg, Thirsk, North Yorkshire, but *not* Bradford or Leeds

(West Yorkshire). Note the **Yorkshire Dales**, or simply the Dales, and the **North York Moors** (not North Yorkshire Moors). But also note **North Yorkshire Moors Railway**

young offender institution l/c for general use, cap for specific, as in Feltham Young Offender Institution

Young Turks (caps)

youth courts, not juvenile courts, which no longer exist. *See* Courts special section (page 47)

yuan, the Chinese currency, rather than the renminbi

Yugoslav is the adjective from Yugoslavia (not Yugoslavian). Write Yugoslav Army, not Serb Army

yuletide (l/c)

yuppie, noun or adjective

Yves Saint Laurent (not St)

Z

Zahir Shah, the returned Afghan King; King Zahir at subsequent mention. *See* War on Terror

Zaire after the overthrow of President Mobutu in May 1997, we should now call the country, at first mention, the Democratic Republic of Congo (formerly Zaire), and thereafter simply Congo. The former French Congo should be called Congo-Brazzaville

Zambezi (not Zambesi)

Zanu (PF) (not Zanu-PF) party in Zimbabwe

-ze in almost all cases use the **-ise** ending rather than the -ize. Two of the main exceptions are *capsize* and *synthesizer*

Zeitgeist (cap, italic), means the spirit of the times

zeppelin (l/c for the airship)

zeros (prefer to zeroes as plural)

Zeta-Jones, Catherine (hyphen)

ziggurat

zigzag, **zigzagging**

Zimmer frame is a trademark, so cap

zodiac, **zodiacal** (l/c, as in signs of the zodiac)

zoo cap as in London Zoo, Dudley Zoo; thereafter, the zoo